Ultimate Laravel for Modern Web Development

Build Robust and Interactive Enterprise-Grade
Web Apps Using Laravel's MVC,
Authentication, APIs, and
Cloud Deployment

Drishti Jain

www.orangeava.com

First published: January 2024
Published by: Orange Education Pvt Ltd, AVA™
Address: 9, Daryaganj, Delhi, 110002

ISBN: 978-81-96782-65-8
www.orangeava.com

Dedicated To

My beloved Mom:

Barkha Jain

My Strength and Support System

About the Author

Drishti Jain holds a Master of Science in Computer Science from the Georgia Institute of Technology, USA, and a Bachelor of Engineering in Computer Engineering from Cummins College of Engineering, Pune, India. She earned the title of the Best Outgoing Student in Computer Engineering for her graduating batch and is acknowledged on the list of award recipients at her institute. She has worked at top product-based companies and FinTech organizations, along with working towards democratizing opportunities and knowledge through her initiative SkillUp with Drishti and her non-profit organization, the Samyak Drishti Foundation.

She is an acclaimed international tech speaker and has spoken at over 100 tech conferences worldwide, including technical conferences in the USA, UK, Europe, Singapore, Colombia, Thailand, Brazil, and India. Actively engaged in the Laravel Ecosystem, she has been invited as a speaker at LARACON, sharing the platform with the core Laravel team along with the creator of Laravel as well as the Laravel India Podcast. Her contributions to the PHP ecosystem are many, including speaking at conferences such as PHP UK, Scotland PHP, and PHP[TEK] in the USA, as well as participating in PHPConf.Asia in Singapore.

She is active in the tech community and frequently shares her knowledge through various blogs, tutorials, seminars, talks, and online posts on social media. You can find her on Twitter/X at @drishtijjain. Beyond her tech pursuits, Drishti is actively involved in environmental conservation and has been felicitated thrice by the Government of Maharashtra, India, with the title 'Eco-Warrior'. Also, she leads a team of over 400 volunteers across the country.

When not working on technical projects, Drishti enjoys canvas painting and exploring new places.

About the Technical Reviewer

Shailesh Davara is a software developer with over 15 years of experience across various domains of software development, both at the personal and team levels. His expertise spans a multitude of technologies.

At Improwised Technologies, Shailesh contributed to the development of Laravel Web Application, starting with version 3.x, during which he was actively involved in coding. In addition to his professional experience, Shailesh is a City Lead and Volunteer in the Laravel community. He also runs a small tech group at Rajkot Tech, fostering collaborative learning and knowledge sharing.

Shailesh expresses gratitude to his colleague, Munir, who played a pivotal role in the review and was instrumental in his journey. He also extends thanks to his partner and friend, Rakshit, for providing valuable assistance in reviewing his work at various points.

For a more detailed overview of Shailesh's professional journey, please visit his LinkedIn profile: https://www.linkedin.com/in/sdavara/

Acknowledgements

Embarking on the journey of writing Modern Web App Development with Laravel has been a wonderful journey, and I am deeply grateful to the individuals who have played a crucial role in bringing this book to fruition. This endeavor wouldn't have been possible without the unwavering support, guidance, and expertise generously shared by many.

Firstly, my heartfelt thanks go to the Laravel community and Taylor Otwell, the creator of Laravel, whose dedication to the framework has shaped this book. The Laravel documentation, an invaluable resource at www.laravel.com/docs, served as a guiding light, enriching the content and ensuring accuracy. Special gratitude is extended to the technical reviewers whose meticulous reviews and insightful feedback enhanced the book. Their dedication and expertise have been invaluable in refining the content and ensuring its accuracy.

To my family, thank you for your unwavering support. In particular, I want to express deep appreciation to my mother, Barkha Jain, whose encouragement and understanding have been a constant source of strength throughout this writing journey. Special thanks to my brother, Samyak Jain, for his steadfast support throughout this endeavor.

To all those at the publication house who have contributed in various capacities, your collective efforts have enriched this endeavor. I appreciate the collaborative spirit that has fueled the creation of Modern Web App Development with Laravel.

Finally, to the readers, thank you for choosing this book as your source of knowledge. May it be a valuable companion on your journey to mastering Laravel and navigating the dynamic world of web development.

Preface

In the fast-evolving landscape of web development, embracing a framework that seamlessly blends power with elegance is paramount. Welcome to *Ultimate Laravel for Modern Web Development* - a journey that transcends the ordinary and propels you into the extraordinary realm of Laravel, a PHP framework that has etched its name as a cornerstone in modern web development.

This book comprises 10 chapters, each a complete module in itself, serving as your comprehensive guide to mastering Laravel. It covers a wide array of topics, ranging from the fundamentals to advanced techniques. Whether you're a seasoned developer looking to expand your skills or a newcomer eager to dive into web development, this book has something for everyone.

Getting Started with Laravel: The chapter sets the stage by introducing you to the framework's core concepts, discussing its significance in web development, and guiding you through the installation and setup process. Learn about the latest version release changes, explore Laravel Artisan, and gain insights into upgrading your applications seamlessly.

MVC Architecture in Laravel: The chapter delves into the Model-View-Controller (MVC) architecture, unraveling its importance in web development. Understand how Laravel adheres to MVC principles and explore controllers, models, and views in depth. Discover key features and design patterns that make Laravel an exceptional framework.

Routers and Views in Laravel: The chapter takes you on a journey through Laravel's routers and views, essential components in web development. Uncover the intricacies of routers, including optional parameters, route groups, and cross-origin resource sharing. Learn how to create and optimize views, enhancing your ability to craft dynamic and engaging web applications.

Building Controllers and Blade Templates: The chapter explores controllers and Blade, pivotal elements in Laravel development. Dive into resource controllers, redirects, directives, and Blade templating. Gain a deep understanding of how these components work together to create robust and maintainable web applications.

Working with Eloquent ORM and Query Builder: The chapter demystifies database operations with Eloquent and Query Builder. Learn to perform common Eloquent operations, utilize query builder methods, and understand the conventions and events that make Laravel's database interactions seamless.

Implementing Authentication and Authorization in Laravel: The chapter equips you with the knowledge to handle user authentication, implement authorization policies, and secure your application. Explore Laravel's built-in authentication system, customize logic, and implement best practices for user data security.

Developing APIs with Laravel: The chapter takes you into the realm of API development. From understanding REST APIs to exploring Laravel Passport, this chapter provides the tools to create robust and scalable APIs for your applications.

Testing and Debugging your Laravel Application: The chapter guides you through the essential practices of testing and debugging in Laravel. Explore the testing lifecycle, HTTP tests, and effective debugging techniques to ensure the reliability and stability of your applications.

E-mail and Notifications in Laravel: The chapter focuses on Laravel's e-mail and notification features. Learn to generate and send notifications, customize email components, and explore broadcast notifications for real-time communication.

Deploying Your Laravel App to Cloud: The chapter concludes the journey by teaching you how to deploy your Laravel application to the Cloud. Understand the fundamentals of Cloud deployment, explore different Cloud providers, and master the use of Laravel Vapor for efficient and scalable deployment.

This book is a hands-on guide filled with practical examples, real-world scenarios, and best practices. I hope this journey through Laravel empowers you to build cutting-edge web applications and enhances your skills in the dynamic field of web development. Happy coding!

Downloading the code bundles and colored images

Please follow the links or scan the QR codes to download the
Code Bundles and Images of the book:

https://github.com/ava-orange-education/Ultimate-Laravel-for-Modern-Web-Development

The code bundles and images of the book are also hosted on
https://rebrand.ly/921f7e

In case there's an update to the code, it will be updated on the existing
GitHub repository.

Errata

We take immense pride in our work at **Orange Education Pvt Ltd,** and follow best practices to ensure the accuracy of our content to provide an indulging reading experience to our subscribers. Our readers are our mirrors, and we use their inputs to reflect and improve upon human errors, if any, that may have occurred during the publishing processes involved. To let us maintain the quality and help us reach out to any readers who might be having difficulties due to any unforeseen errors, please write to us at :

errata@orangeava.com

Your support, suggestions, and feedback are highly appreciated.

DID YOU KNOW

Did you know that Orange Education Pvt Ltd offers eBook versions of every book published, with PDF and ePub files available? You can upgrade to the eBook version at **www.orangeava.com** and as a print book customer, you are entitled to a discount on the eBook copy. Get in touch with us at: **info@orangeava.com** for more details.

At **www.orangeava.com**, you can also read a collection of free technical articles, sign up for a range of free newsletters, and receive exclusive discounts and offers on AVA™ Books and eBooks.

PIRACY

If you come across any illegal copies of our works in any form on the internet, we would be grateful if you would provide us with the location address or website name. Please contact us at **info@orangeava.com** with a link to the material.

ARE YOU INTERESTED IN AUTHORING WITH US?

If there is a topic that you have expertise in, and you are interested in either writing or contributing to a book, please write to us at **business@orangeava.com**. We are on a journey to help developers and tech professionals to gain insights on the present technological advancements and innovations happening across the globe and build a community that believes Knowledge is best acquired by sharing and learning with others. Please reach out to us to learn what our audience demands and how you can be part of this educational reform. We also welcome ideas from tech experts and help them build learning and development content for their domains.

REVIEWS

Please leave a review. Once you have read and used this book, why not leave a review on the site that you purchased it from? Potential readers can then see and use your unbiased opinion to make purchase decisions. We at Orange Education would love to know what you think about our products, and our authors can learn from your feedback. Thank you!

For more information about Orange Education, please visit **www.orangeava.com**.

Table of Contents

1. Getting Started with Laravel..1

   Introduction..1

   Structure..1

   Introduction to Laravel 2

       Preference for Laravel..2

       Scalable...2

       MVC Architecture..2

       Community...3

       Class Dependency Management 3

       Eloquent ORM...3

       Unique Features of Laravel...5

       Database Seeding...5

       Localization...6

   Latest Version Release Changes 8

       How to Upgrade 8

       Dependencies 8

           Minimum Stability...9

           Public Path Binding 9

           Redis Cache Tags 10

           Database Expressions 10

           Eloquent...10

           Testing...11

   Installation and Setup of Laravel Development Environment 11

       Installing PHP..11

       Mac..11

       Windows..12

       Installing Composer...14

       Mac..14

Windows..16

Installing Laravel..17

Laravel Artisan..18

Core Concept..24

Conclusion..25

2. MVC Architecture in Laravel..**26**

Introduction..26

Structure..26

Overview of MVC Architecture..26

History..27

Separation of Components..27

MVC Architecture Pattern in the Context of Laravel................28

Design Principles..29

Reusability..29

Flexibility..29

Cohesion..29

Coupling..30

Design Independence in Components................................30

MVC in Laravel..30

Key Features..31

SEO Friendly..31

Importance of SEO..31

Principles..31

Test Driven Development..32

Simultaneous Development..32

Maintainability and Extensibility................................32

Models in Laravel..33

Views in Laravel..33

Controllers in Laravel..34

Conclusion..34

3. Routers and Views in Laravel **36**

   Introduction 36

   Structure...36

   Routers in Laravel 37

      Introduction to Routers 37

      Routes Directory 38

      Router Methods 39

      Types of Routers... 39

      Redirect Routes 40

      View Routes 40

      The Route List 40

      Fallback Routes 41

      Route Parameters 41

      Optional Parameters 42

      Regular Expressions Constraints 43

      Regular Expressions... 43

         Regular Expressions Constraints 45

      Route Groups 46

      Middleware..47

      Controllers.. 48

      Subdomain Routing.. 49

      Route Prefixes 49

      Cross-origin Resource Sharing (CORS)................................50

      Caching.. 51

   Views in Laravel 51

      Creating Views... 52

      Views and View Extensions.. 53

      Nested Views Directories 53

      First Available View 53

      Data and Views 54

      Sharing Data... 55

View Composers and Creators 56

View Composers 56

Multiple Views with Composer 59

View Creators 60

View Optimization 60

Conclusion 61

Points to Remember 62

4. Building Controllers and Blade Templates **63**

Introduction 63

Structure 63

Controllers with Views in Laravel 64

Controllers 64

Resource Controllers 65

Constructor Injection 67

Method Injection 68

Redirects in Laravel 69

Redirect Helper 69

Redirecting to Named Routes 69

Redirecting to Controller Actions 70

Redirecting - Flashed Session Data 70

Directives in Laravel 71

Conditional Directives 72

Custom if Statements 73

Switch Directive 73

Auth Directive 74

Loops 76

Once Directive 78

Blade as Template Engines in Laravel 79

Data in Blade 79

HTML Entity Encoding 80

Components 81

Rendering Components 82

       Passing Data..83

       Layouts..84

       Template Inheritance...85

       Rendering Blade Templates..86

       Rendering Blade Fragments...87

    Conclusion 88

    Points to Remember 88

5. Working with Eloquent ORM and Query Builder.........................**90**

    Introduction 90

    Structure..90

    Eloquent in Laravel...91

       Database Migrations 92

          Primary Key 93

       Timestamps 94

    Eloquent Events 95

    Query Builder in Laravel 97

       Selects..97

       Joins 99

       Left Join..99

       Advanced Joins 100

       Advanced Where 100

       Aggregates..101

       Raw Expressions 101

       Pessimistic Locking 102

       Caching Queries 102

    Eloquent Operations...102

       Model Classes 103

       Model Conventions 104

       Table Name 105

       Primary Key..105

       UUID and ULID Keys...108

       Database Connections..110

Retrieving Models...110

Collections...111

Chunking Results..112

Chunk Using Lazy Collections..113

Cursors...114

Advanced Subqueries..115

CRUD Operations on Models...116

Events...118

Conclusion..120

Points to Remember 121

6. Implementing Authentication and Authorization in Laravel.............122

Introduction 122

Structure..122

Laravel's built-in Authentication System...123

Laravel API Authentication Services...124

Passport...124

Sanctum..125

Customizing Authentication and Registration logic...........................125

HTTP Authentication 125

Stateless HTTP Authentication 126

Custom User Providers 127

User Provider Contract...129

Authenticatable Contract..131

Implementing Authorization Policies and Gates 132

Invalidating User Sessions..133

Password Management..134

Configuration 134

Routing..134

Authentication Custom Guards 136

Closure Request Guards..137

Invalidate Sessions across Multiple Devices 139

User Session Knowledge 140

Additional Authentication Methods...140

Authenticate a User Instance...141

Authenticate a User By ID..142

Authenticate a User Once 142

Securing Routes and Actions with Middleware 142

Middleware...143

Assigning Middleware To Routes...146

Middleware Groups 148

Sorting Middleware...150

Middleware Parameters 151

Terminable Middleware 152

Conclusion...154

Points to Remember 155

7. **Developing APIs with Laravel**...**156**

Introduction 156

Structure..156

Understanding APIs, REST 157

REST 157

SOAP 157

Resources, Collections and Nesting Relationships 157

Writing Resource 161

Relationships...162

Data Wrapping..163

Understanding Data Wrapping 165

Conditional Relationships...167

Resource Response...169

Laravel Passport...170

Installing and Setup..171

Configuration 172

Token Lifetimes..172

Overriding Default Models 173

Overriding Routes...174

Access Tokens..175

    Client...175

    JSON API...176

        GET..176

        POST..177

        PUT..177

        DELETE...178

    Protecting Routes..178

    Middleware...179

    Access Token..180

    Token Scopes..180

    Defining a scope...180

    Default Scope..181

        Check Scope..182

Conclusion..183

Points to Remember 184

8. Testing and Debugging your Laravel Application **185**

Introduction...185

Structure...185

Introduction to Testing in Laravel..186

    Setting up Environment for Testing...186

    Testing Lifecycle..187

        Creating Tests...187

        Running Tests...189

        Parallel Execution of Tests...189

        Reporting..192

HTTP Tests 193

    Make a Request..193

    Customizing Request Headers 194

        Cookies..195

        Authentication..196

        Debugging Responses 198

Exception Handling 200

File Upload Testing 200

Debugging in Laravel 202

Conclusion 203

Points to Remember 204

9. E-mail and Notifications in Laravel **205**

Introduction 205

Structure 205

Generating Notifications 206

Sending Notifications 206

    Delivery Channels 207

    Queuing Notifications 208

    Delaying Notifications 209

    Custom Notification Queue 210

    Custom Notification Channel Queue 211

    On-Demand Notifications 213

Mail Notifications 214

    Customizing Email Components 215

    Custom templates 217

        Handling Raw Data 219

    Tags and Metadata 220

    Custom Symfony Message 221

Broadcast Notifications 221

    Notification Events 224

Conclusion 226

Points to Remember 227

10. Deploying your Laravel App to Cloud **229**

Introduction 229

Structure 229

Cloud Deployment Fundamentals 230

Cloud Providers Overview 231

    Amazon Web Services 231

Heroku..232

Google Cloud 232

Laravel Application Deployment with Vapor 233

Installation 233

Installing the Vapor Core 234

Installing the Vapor Dashboard 234

Dashboard Authorization.. 235

Environment.. 235

Deployment 239

Hooks.. 239

Development 241

Configure OpenSSL 241

Domains 244

DNS Records.. 245

Custom Records... 245

SSL Certificates.. 246

Add Domain to Environment.. 246

Troubleshooting...249

Conclusion...250

Points to Remember 251

Index **252**

CHAPTER 1

Getting Started with Laravel

Introduction

This chapter provides an overview of Laravel and its importance in web development. It discusses the features and benefits of using Laravel as a web development framework. The chapter also explains the major changes in the latest Laravel version release and how to upgrade existing Laravel applications. Additionally, the chapter discusses the key pillars of Laravel and what makes it a powerful framework for web development. Laravel Artisan, the CLI of Laravel, is also discussed in depth.

Structure

In this chapter, we will cover the following topics:

- Introduction to Laravel
- Preference for Laravel
- Latest Version Release Changes
  - How to Upgrade
- Installation and Setup of Laravel Development Environment
  - Mac
  - Windows
- Laravel Artisan
  - Overview and History
  - Commands
- Core Concept

Introduction to Laravel

Laravel is a web application development framework based on the PHP programming language. It is an open-source framework designed to make it easy for developers to build high-quality web applications quickly and efficiently.

Laravel provides a rich set of features that simplify the development process and allow developers to focus on the core functionality of their applications. The framework is well-suited for both novice users in the world of web development and experts in the field of development.

Laravel is a PHP web framework that provides capabilities for building modern, full-stack web applications.

It is an open-source framework, and its document is available at https://www.laravel.com/

Preference for Laravel

In the ever-moving technology landscape, numerous frameworks come into the market. In this section of the chapter, we will explore what makes Laravel unique and stand out among other frameworks for application development.

Scalable

PHP is a scalable language, and Laravel provides built-in support for fast, distributed cache systems like Redis, making the framework support horizontal scalability. Laravel applications in the past have been able to scale to handle hundreds of millions of requests per month.

Laravel platforms, such as Laravel Vapor, provide serverless capabilities for Laravel development. It is powered with Amazon Web Services (AWS) and makes including capabilities of AWS in Laravel development easy and maintainable.

MVC Architecture

The Laravel framework is based on the Model-View-Controller pattern (MVC pattern), which makes the application's business logic and presentation to be distinct, making the framework powerful by increasing its performance. This concept is discussed in-depth in *Chapter 2, MVC Architecture in Laravel,* In this book.

Community

Laravel has a robust and active community. The project is open-source and has active contributors, discussion forums, and a strong developer community. The strength of the Laravel community enables new developers of the framework to find good documentation and makes it easy for them to learn and develop using Laravel. Additionally, Laravel is adopted by many developers, leading to increased demand and support in case of issues during development. This lowers the barrier to entry for novice developers and fosters a welcoming and supportive environment.

Class Dependency Management

Laravel framework is powered by the Inversion of Control Container (IoC Container), which enables class dependency management. It makes the framework powerful by its capability to automatically resolve classes without configuration.

The dependencies are tackled at runtime, which allows flexibility as dependency implementations can be swapped easily. The two ways in which the IoC container can resolve dependencies are Closure callbacks and automatic resolution.

Eloquent ORM

Laravel framework enables Eloquent Object-Relational Mapping (ORM), allowing Laravel developers to write with PHP syntax over SQL syntax. It provides a great and optimal way of implementation of `ActiveRecord` for working with one's application database. Eloquent ORM is explored more in *Chapter 5, Working with Eloquent ORM and Query Builder*, of the book.

Laravel is a powerful, robust, and developer-friendly framework, providing modern capabilities to develop applications. *Figure 1.1* highlights the key pillars of Laravel that make developers prefer it.

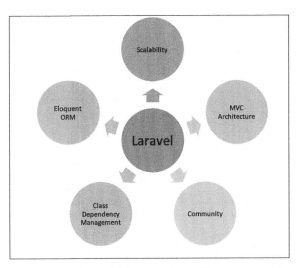

Figure 1.1: Laravel Key Pillars

Laravel also provides the following capabilities:

- **URL Routing Configuration**

  This enables viewing the content of a link in the same webpage instead of redirecting to the link. With Laravel's built-in file configuration, it is loaded with the framework and provides a seamless experience for the application user.

- **Mail Service**

  Laravel has the `Swiftmailer` library, which enables clean and straightforward API configurations for individual email accounts. It provides drivers to permit message sending via cloud-based and local services.

  Some of the drivers include SMTP, Mailgun, Mandrill, SparkPost, PHP's `mail` and `Sendmail` functions, and Amazon SES.

- **Message Queue System**

  Laravel enables and powers the message queue system with its own built-in queue system, which is a simple API capable of running tasks in the background. It also supports message queues like Redis, SQS, and many more.

- **Scheduling**

  Laravel provides the capability to custom schedule tasks and jobs without requiring the developer to set it up at the system level. The Laravel CRON job is Laravel's built-in utility that provides scheduling functionality in a user-friendly way.

- **Authentication and Authorization**

  The key factor that makes the Laravel framework loved by developers is the ability to enable easy control access to resources and organize authentication logic.

  Laravel site owners can seamlessly streamline authentication, and the framework provides the owners with flexibility and security when dealing with authorization and authentication.

Unique Features of Laravel

Laravel is widely adopted across the developer ecosystem and has become the go-to framework for developers for their application development. What makes Laravel unique are its several diverse features. Let's explore these unique features of Laravel.

Database Seeding

The Laravel framework has the ability to populate the database tables with seed data using seed classes. These seed classes are stored in the **database/seeders** directory, with a default **DatabaseSeeder** class defined.

This class can be modified to the application's requirement.

Let's write an example of the **DatabaseSeeder** class to add plants and their species name:

```php
<?php

namespace Database\Seeders;
use Illuminate\Database\Seeder;
use Illuminate\Support\Facades\DB;
use Illuminate\Support\Str;

class DatabaseSeeder extends Seeder
{
    /**
```

```
 * Run the database seeders.
 */
public function run(): void
{
    DB::table('plants')->insert([
        'name' => Str::random(10),
        'species' => Str::random(10)
    ]);
}
}
```

Localization

With globalization and to accommodate users across the globe with different languages, Laravel provides the localization feature, enabling the retrieval of strings in different languages. This allows the Laravel application to support multiple languages within the Laravel application.

There are two ways to achieve translation strings:

- **lang directory**

    The language strings must be stored in the **lang** directory. There is also support to include subdirectories for each language supported by the application. Through this feature, Laravel can manage translation strings for built-in features, such as validation error messages.

    ```
    /lang
        /en
            messages.php
        /es
            messages.php
    ```

- **JSON files**

    Translation strings can also be placed within JSON files, which must be stored in the **lang** directory structure. In this approach, each of the application's supported languages will be in a separate JSON file, which will be listed under the **lang** directory.

When dealing with a large number of translation strings, this method must be preferred.

```
/lang
    en.json
    es.json
```

Configuring the locale is also trivial in this case. By default, the application's default language is stored in the **config/app.php** configuration file under the **locale** configuration option.

The default language can be modified for a single HTTP request at runtime with the **setLocale** method of the **App** facade.

```
use Illuminate\Support\Facades\App;

Route::get('/greeting/{locale}', function (string $locale) {
    if (! in_array($locale, ['en', 'es'])) {
        abort(400);
    }

    App::setLocale($locale);

    // ...
});
```

It is also a good practice to configure a fallback language. This should be configured in the **config/app.php** configuration file.

The syntax to set a fallback language is as follows:

```
'falback_locale' => '<language>'
```

An example, to set the fallback language as English:

'falback_locale' => 'en'

To determine the current locale, the **currentLocale** and **isLocale** methods can be used, as follows:

```
use Illuminate\Support\Facades\App;

$locale = App::currentLocale();

if (App::isLocale('es')) {
    // ...
}
```

Latest Version Release Changes

Laravel 10 is the current Laravel version in use. If you already have a previous version of Laravel, you can continue to upgrade it. Alternatively, if you are new, follow the next section of the chapter on how to install Laravel.

How to Upgrade

In order to upgrade any existing Laravel projects to Laravel 10, updating the dependencies is the most crucial step. The documentation for the upgrade is available at https://laravel.com/docs/10.x/upgrade

Let's explore how to upgrade to Laravel 10 to get the latest features and make the necessary changes to upgrade our existing Laravel applications.

Dependencies

Laravel requires PHP 8.1.0 or higher and Composer version 2.20 or higher.

The following dependencies need to be upgraded in the Laravel applications `composer.json` file:

Dependency	Version
laravel/framework	^10.0
laravel/sanctum	^3.2
doctrine/dbal	^3.0
spatie/laravel-ignition	^2.0
laravel/passport	^11.0

Table 1.1: `composer.json` dependencies for Laravel 10

Additionally, if you wish to use PHPUnit 10, then delete the `processUncoveredFiles` attribute from the `<coverage>` section of `phpunit.xml`, and update the following in the `composer.json` file:

Dependency	Version
nunomaduro/collision	^7.0
phpunit/phpunit	^10.0

Table 1.2: `composer.json` dependencies for Laravel 10 if using PHPUnit 10

Furthermore, verify support for any other third-party packages used in your application with Laravel 10.

Minimum Stability

The `minimum-stability` setting in the `composer.json` needs to be set to the value `stable`:

```
"minimum-stability": "stable",
```

The default value of `minimum-stability` is now stable; so you may also choose to remove this completely.

Public Path Binding

Update your code in your Laravel application to invoke the `usePublicPath` method of the `Illuminate\Foundation\Application` object. This should be done instead of customizing its **public path** binding to **path.public** into the container:

```
app()->usePublicPath(__DIR__.'/public');
```

Redis Cache Tags

The Redis cache tag has been rewritten in the Laravel version update for better performance and efficient storage capabilities. Laravel has a new **cache:prune-stale-tags** Artisan command that needs to be scheduled in the application's **App\Console\Kernel** class:

```
$schedule->command('cache:prune-stale-tags')->hourly();
```

```
Adding the above scheduled job will corporate the latest update.
```

Database Expressions

The database expressions have been rewritten in Laravel 10 to make it possible to add functionalities in the future.

The following method and the manual casting need to be replaced with the **getValue** method:

- Manual casting using **(string)**
- _ _**toString** method

Casting expression using the **(string)** is not supported in this version.

Eloquent

The **$dates** property of the Eloquent model is deprecated. The application should update the instances with the **$casts** property.

For example:

```
protected $casts = [
        'deployed_at' => 'datetime',
    ];
```

Testing

The `MocksApplicationServices` trait is removed and deprecated.

The trait provided the following methods:

- `expectsEvents`
- `expectsJobs`
- `expectsNotifications`

These have to be replaced with the following methods (in order):

- ○ `Event::fake`
- ○ `Bus::fake`
- ○ `Notification::fake`

The Language Directory

The Laravel application skeleton does not support the `lang` directory. Any new Laravel applications can be published using the `lang:publish` command as follows:

```
php artisan lang:publish
```

Installation and Setup of Laravel Development Environment

In this section, we will look at the setup of the Laravel development based on the operating system of the machine. For the three commonly used operating systems – Windows, Mac, and Linux – the requirement is to have PHP and Composer installed on the machine.

Installing PHP

We will guide you through the process of installing PHP on both Mac and Windows systems.

Mac

To install PHP on a Mac machine, Homebrew provides a direct and easy way to install PHP.

To install Homebrew on the machine, visit www.brew.sh and follow the instructions.

Alternatively, you can run the following command on the terminal to install Homebrew:

```
/bin/bash -c
"$(curl -fsSL https://raw.githubusercontent.com/Homebrew/install/HEAD/
install.sh)"
```

Next, run the following command to install PHP:

```
brew install php
```

This will install the latest PHP version on the machine and also take care of any environment variable settings, and setting the PATH on the machine.

Windows

The following steps will enable you to install PHP on a Windows machine:

1. Visit the **Downloads** section on www.php.net

Figure 1.2: Downloads Section on www.php.net

2. Select **Windows Downloads**.

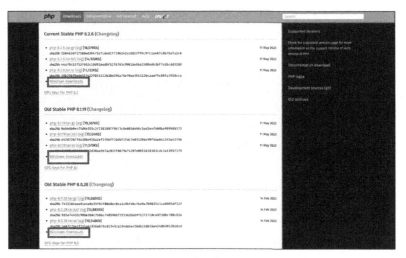

Figure 1.3: *Windows Download Section on www.php.net*

3. Download the thread-safe version:

   It is imperative to select the thread-safe version. The thread-safe version for PHP 8.2 is highlighted with the blue box in *Figure* 1.4:

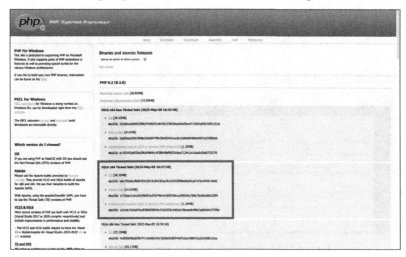

Figure 1.4: *Thread-safe PHP version*

4. Extract the downloaded file.

5. Copy the extracted folder to the **Program Files** folder on your machine.

6. Allow Windows the permission to paste the extracted folder.

Setting the environment variable:

1. Copy the address of the folder in the **Program Files** of the folder above.

2. Click the **Start** Menu and open **Edit the system environment variables**.

3. Click **Environment Variables**.

4. Navigate to **System Variables** and **Edit** the PATH variable.

5. Add the copied address from above by selecting **New** and pasting the address of the extracted folder in **Program Files**.

6. Click **OK** to add, and then click **OK** to save changes.

PHP is now successfully installed on your Windows machine.

To verify the installation of PHP, open the command prompt and check the version of PHP installed by running the following command:

```
php -v
```

The command prompt should now display the version of PHP installed, indicating a successful installation.

Installing Composer

The dependency required to be installed after PHP is Composer. Based on the operating system you are using, follow the steps to install Composer.

Mac

To install Composer on Mac, there are two methods – via Installer and via Homebrew. Let's explore both methods.

Via Homebrew

To install Composer on a Mac machine, Homebrew provides a direct and easy way to install Composer.

If you have already installed Homebrew (as explained in the previous step for installing PHP), then you can skip this Homebrew installation step.

To install Homebrew on the machine, visit www.brew.sh and follow the instructions.

To install Composer via Homebrew, run the following command:

```
brew install composer
```

This will install the latest composer version on the machine and also take care of any environment variable settings, and setting the PATH on the machine.

To install a specific version of Composer, run the following command:

```
brew install composer@<versionNumber>
```

Replace **versionNumber** with the desired Composer Version number.

Via Installer

Perform the following steps to install Composer via the installer on Mac:

1. Download the installer.

    Run the following command on the terminal to download the latest version of Composer on Mac:

    ```
    sudo php -r "copy('https://getcomposer.org/installer',' composer-setup.php');"
    ```

2. Verify installer via Hash

    Run the following command to verify the authenticity of the installer:

    ```
    php -r «if (hash_file('sha384', 'composer setup.php') === '756890a4488ce9024fc62c56153228907f1545 c228516cbf63f885e036d37e9a59d27d63f46af1d4d07ee0f76181c7d3') { echo 'Installer verified'; } else { echo 'Installer corrupt'; unlink('composer-setup.php'); }"
    ```

3. Run the setup.

    Run the setup file of Composer via the terminal using the following command:

    ```
    php composer-setup.php
    ```

4. Move the Phar file to **/usr/bin/composer**:

    ```
    sudo mv composer.phar /usr/local/bin/composer
    ```

5. Run Composer.

    Type the following on the terminal to run Composer:

    ```
    composer
    ```

The Composer version and help menu will be displayed, indicating Composer is now successfully installed.

Windows

Perform the following steps to install Composer on Windows:

1. Go to www.getcomposer.org

2. Click **Download** on the Composer website.

3. Download **Composer-Setup.exe file**.

4. Select **Install for all users**.

5. Let the default settings be selected or choose the options as prompted.

6. Wait for the installation to complete and click **Finish**.

Composer is now successfully installed on your Windows machine. To verify the installation of Composer, open the command prompt and run the following command:

```
composer
```

The output will display the version of the Composer installed, and you will be able to verify the successful installation of the Composer.

Installing Laravel

Once PHP and Composer are installed on the system, the steps to install Laravel are straightforward for both platforms.

Via Installer

To install Laravel using the installer, we make use of Composer.

Run the following command on the terminal to download the Laravel installer:

```
composer global require laravel/installer
```

Once the installation is complete, the `new` command is used to create a fresh installation of Laravel in the desired directory. The command for the same is as follows:

```
laravel new directoryName
```

It is important to make sure that the composer's system-wide vendor bin is added as a part of the PATH variable on your system. The directory location can be found using the following command:

```
composer global about
```

Generally, the common locations based on the operating systems are as follows:

Mac

```
$HOME/.composer/vendor/bin
```

Windows

```
%USERPROFILE%\AppData\Roaming\Composer\vendor\bin
```

Linux

```
$HOME/.config/composer/vendor/bin
```

Or

```
$HOME/.composer/vendor/bin
```

Via Composer Create-Project

The Laravel installation can also be done with the **create-project** command of Composer.

Run the following command on your terminal:

```
composer create-project --prefer-dist laravel/laravel:^10.0 blog
```

Via PHP serve

Laravel can also be run with PHP's built-in development server. The **serve Artisan** command is used for the same.

Run the following command on your terminal:

```
php artisan serve
```

Laravel Artisan

Laravel's command-line interface is **Artisan.** It enables the use of capabilities both on the command line as well as outside CLI.

A Brief History of Artisan

Artisan is the powerful Command-Line Interface (CLI) included with Laravel. It provides powerful and robust capabilities for developers to develop Laravel applications.

The Symphony Console Component is the backbone of Artisan and helps power the capabilities of strong command-line features to easy developer workflow.

Commands

Artisan is included with Laravel and does not require any additional installation. Let's look at some of the commands.

- **Version**

  To check the current Laravel version, run the following command on the terminal:

  ```
  php artisan -version
  ```

- **List**

  The `list` command enables you to view all the available Artisan commands. Use this to your advantage to get the command list on the go. It serves as a dictionary of the Artisan commands and can be accessed anytime on the terminal with the following command:

  ```
  php artisan list
  ```

  This will give you a list of all commands.

- **Help**

  The `help` command enables you to get more information about the command it is used with. Let's look at an example – to understand what the `migrate` command does, use the following:

  ```
  php artisan help migrate
  ```

  Whenever you want to understand what a command does, the arguments available with the command, and the functionality of the command, use the `help` command.

- **Scheduling Commands**

  Laravel provides developers the capability to schedule commands within Laravel itself, requiring only a single CRON entry on the server.

  o   CRON stands for Command Run On

  The command schedule is stored in the `Kernel.php` file located under the `app/Console` directory. The schedule method in this class is used to define as many scheduled jobs as desired with the `schedule` object.

To invoke the Laravel command scheduler every minute, add the following code to the server:

```
* * * * * php /path/to/artisan schedule:run 1>> /dev/null 2>&1
```

This will ensure that the scheduler is called every minute, and then Laravel can take care of the scheduled jobs and run them as per the defined schedule.

- **Frequent Repeating Jobs**

  To schedule a job every five minutes or every ten minutes, the schedule job code will look like the following examples:

  Job Every Five Minutes:

  ```
  $schedule->command('test')->everyFiveMinutes();
  ```

  Job Every Ten Minutes:

  ```
  $schedule->command('test')->everyTenMinutes();
  ```

  Daily Repeating Jobs:

  ```
  $schedule->command('test')->daily();
  ```

  At a Specific Time Daily:

  ```
  $schedule->command('test')->dailyAt('10:00');
  ```

  The preceding command will run the job named **test** at 10 am every day. The time at which the job needs to be triggered every day can be modified by changing the time argument in the **dailyAt()** function.

  This enables load-balance on the server; the schedule of multiple jobs should be non-overlapping so that the server does not become sluggish, and dependent jobs should be scheduled before any dependent jobs are scheduled.

Specific Day Jobs:

The following methods enable to schedule jobs on specific days:

```
mondays()
tuesdays()
wednesdays()
thursdays()
fridays()
saturdays()
sundays()
```

Based on the frequency required of the scheduled jobs on specific days of the week, the corresponding method can be used to schedule the job.

Jobs can be scheduled to run every weekday as well using the following method:

```
weekdays()
```

Weekly Repeating Jobs:

```
$schedule->command('test')->weekly();
```

At a Specific Time Weekly:

```
$schedule->command('test')->weeklyOn(1,'10:00');
```

The first argument of the **weeklyOn()** method is the day of the week the developer wants the scheduled job to run. The second argument of the **weeklyOn()** method is the time of the selected weekday (specified in the first parameter) at which the job should run.

The first parameter takes arguments in the range of 0-6, where each number represents a day of the week. The second argument is the time of the day.

Custom Schedule Jobs:

In order to have more customization and frequency in the schedule of jobs, Laravel allows the same with the manual CRON expression:

```
$schedule->command('test')->cron('* * * * *');
```

Overlapping Jobs Avoidance:

With a number of jobs being scheduled, it is critical that the previously scheduled completes before the same job is retriggered. To handle this overlapping of jobs, Laravel provides a method that can be used in scheduling:

```
$schedule->command('test')->withoutOverlapping();
```

The `withoutOverlapping()` method ensures that the `test` command will run every minute if it not running currently. This ensures there is no overlap in the jobs running.

Isolatable Commands:

When working on developing Laravel Applications, as a developer, multiple commands may run. There will be instances when you want only an instance of the command to run at a given time. In this scenario, the concept of Isolatable Commands comes into the picture.

The Isolatable interface consists of all the core logic required to execute Isolatable Commands. The interface needs to be implemented in the command class to use the functionality.

The interface is located at:

```
Illuminate\Contracts\Console\Isolatable
```

This Isolatable interface is used by the class that will implement the interface using the `implements` keyword.

Let us understand this concept in depth with the following example.

Consider a scenario where a class named `SendNotifications` is to be implemented in such a way that an instance of the class is invoked at any given time in the application. This makes it need the functionality of the `Isolatable` interface.

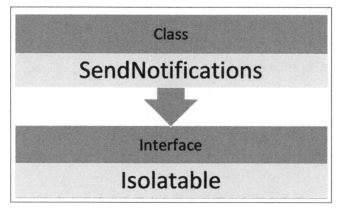

Figure 1.5: *Class **SendNotifications** implements Isolatable Interface*

The code in the PHP class will look as follows:

```php
namespace App\Console\Commands;

use Illuminate\Console\Command;
use Illuminate\Contracts\Console\Isolatable;

class SendNotifications extends Command implements Isolatable
{
    // ...
}
```

As a command is marked as `Isolatable`, Laravel automatically adds the `--isolate` option to the command, reducing the option adding overload from the programmer.

This ensures that the command has only a single instance when it is invoked with the option.

Core Concept

The core concept in the way Laravel is able to achieve the feature of Isolatable on the command and ensure a single instance of the command (and no multiple instances) is by using the underlying default cache driver of the application.

By acquiring an atomic lock using the application's default cache driver, the command is marked as Isolatable.

In a scenario when other instances of the command are already in progress, the **isolatable** marked command will not execute and will exit with a successful exit code by default. It is possible to specify the exit code the command should exit in such a scenario by specifying the desired status code via the **isolate** option in the command.

To specify an exit code of 12 when another instance of the command is already running, specify as follows:

```
--isolated=12
```

Lock Expiry Management

The lock expires in two scenarios, namely:

- The command execution is done, and the lock expires by default.
- The command is interrupted and unable to finish, the lock will expire in 1 hour.

The lock expiration can be modified by defining the **isolationLockExpiresAt()** method on the command.

Let's look at the code for the method:

```
use DateTimeInterface;
use DateInterval;


public function isolationLockExpiresAt(): DateTimeInterface|DateInterval
{
```

```
        return now()->addMinutes(10);
}
```

The aim of the preceding code is to customize the lock expiration time and to set it to add 10 minutes as the expiration of the lock time.

This enables us to base the expiration of the lock based on the business logic of our application. It is key to note that in case we do not custom specify the time when the lock will expire, the two scenarios are by default incorporated and will take care to release the lock in the given time, as mentioned at the start.

Conclusion

In this chapter, we explored what the Laravel framework is, why it is preferred by developers, and its growing adaptability for application development. We discussed the key pillars of Laravel, namely Scalability, MVC architecture, Community, Eloquent ORM, and Class Dependency management. We looked at the pillars and explored what makes these features unique and how they make the Laravel framework powerful.

Next, we learned about upgrading to the latest Laravel version, including the changes required to handle deprecated methods, upgrade to versions of the application dependencies, and also the command replacement required based on the latest Laravel version change.

We looked at the installation steps and system requirements to install Laravel on machines, and the various steps involved based on the operating system of the machine.

Laravel artisan is at the core of everything related to Laravel development. In this chapter, we looked at the history and what Artisan is, explored the commands, and looked at scheduling CRON jobs and automating tasks. Additionally, we explored the optimization technique to handle overlapping scheduled jobs and how to avoid the same. The chapter covered Isolatable commands, emphasizing the need and how to implement them into our Laravel applications.

In the next chapter, we will dive deep into the MVC architecture pattern and how the pattern is used to build Laravel.

## CHAPTER 2

MVC Architecture in Laravel

Introduction

This chapter focuses on the Model-View-Controller (MVC) architectural pattern followed in Laravel. The chapter explores the key properties of MVC used in Laravel application development. It covers practices for writing better code and incorporating key features.

Structure

In this chapter, the focus will be on the following topics:

- Overview of MVC Architecture
- How Laravel Follows the MVC Architecture
  - Design Patterns
- MVC in Laravel
  - Key Features
  - Models in Laravel
  - Views in Laravel
  - Controllers in Laravel

Overview of MVC Architecture

MVC architecture stands for the Model-View-Controller architectural pattern. This is a special architectural pattern that separates an application into distinct logical components, namely model, view, and controller. The logical separation enables the division of different aspects of the application into separate components. These components are handled separately while maintaining the flow of actions between the three components. This ensures the handling of the separate business logic based on the components.

History

The MVC architecture pattern was first introduced in 1979 by Trygve Mikkjel Heyerdahl Reenskaug.

The motivation behind creating the MVC pattern was to divide the complex application into smaller, manageable components. Before the introduction of the MVC architecture pattern, the complexity of handling different actions and tasks made the application less maintainable and took relatively more time to develop the application due to a lack of separation in responsibilities of tasks within the application.

It was then in the late 1970s, while working on Samlltalk-79, Trygve Reenskaug created a pattern (MVC) to overcome this complexity. He aimed to create a pattern to be used to structure applications used by users who interacted with large amounts of data.

The original name of the pattern was going to be Model-View-Editor, but it was changed to Model-View-Controller.

In the early years of the adoption of the MVC pattern, it was used in desktop applications. Towards the late 1990s, it became popular with web applications and led to becoming a common industry favorite for developing web applications. The boom of the internet and business going digital fueled the wide adoption of the MVC architectural pattern in applications.

Separation of Components

The MVC architectural pattern separates the three major responsibilities into three components as shown in *Figure 2.1*:

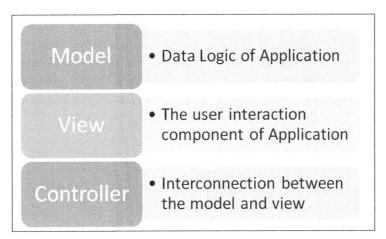

Figure 2.1: *MVC Separation of Components*

MVC Architecture Pattern in the Context of Laravel

The MVC architecture pattern enables Laravel to use the powerful capabilities of the pattern. With the MVC architecture pattern, the key distinction is the division of the logical components, which makes the application code base modular and efficient for making changes – adding or removing features.

There are several design principles that our Laravel application adheres to as it uses the MVC architecture pattern.

Consider the Model in Laravel to be the brains behind your data. It employs Eloquent ORM, which is similar to the language used for communicating with the database. So, when you wish to deal with your database in a more structured manner, Eloquent can assist you by employing syntax that is similar to talking to the database in a human-friendly manner.

Consider the View to be the front face of your application. We employ Blade Templates in Laravel, which are blueprints for how your web pages should look. They maintain the HTML structure and ensure that everything is properly shown to the user.

Controllers are in charge of the entire process. They act as intermediaries between the Model and the View. The Controllers intervene when a user performs an action on the website, such as clicking a button or completing a form. They communicate with the Model to get or modify data and then transfer that data to the View to display to the user what they want.

Finally, Resources and Collections in Laravel are data management wizards. Consider RESTful resource controllers to be your assistants while doing CRUD activities such as adding, viewing, updating, or removing data. They offer unique methods for each of these responsibilities, making data handling in your application simple. As a result, it's similar to having a set of tools to handle various parts of your data in a systematic manner.

Design Principles

The core feature of Laravel lies in optimally using the Design Principles. Let us explore the Design Principles and how they power Laravel.

Reusability

The MVC architecture makes the code into separate logical components. The distinction in capabilities and components allows for the creation of components that can be reused directly.

The controller and view extensively make use of the reusability principle, and the components created in both the view and controller are majorly reused for user interface components.

Flexibility

The MVC architecture focuses on designing the application with a focus on flexibility. With the distinction in the logical components of model, view, and controller, it is relatively easy to make changes and incorporate new behaviors and workflows into the existing application.

It gives the developer the freedom to change the view or the controller or both easily without having drastic changes in the model and sometimes with no changes needed in the model. This makes Laravel application development flexible.

Cohesion

The components of the model, view, and controller in the architecture pattern have a strong layer cohesion. In comparison to when there is no logical separation of the component's responsibilities, having the MVC architecture enforces cohesion between the three components.

Coupling

The three components of the MVC architecture pattern have a logical separation, and it may seem that inter-component communication might be impacted by this pattern. However, the opposite is true.

The communication channels between these channels are efficient and very minimal, leading to a quick transfer of data and information between the components. This leads to smooth and easy transfer of data between the components and also reduces coupling, resulting in increased performance of the application system.

Design Independence in Components

The components are separated with the MVC architecture pattern, making the designing of each component to be separate and independent. This helps to use different and varied design strategies for each of the components very well.

The logical separation of the components also gives the developer the ability to incorporate best design practices in each component, making it optimal for the task each component performs.

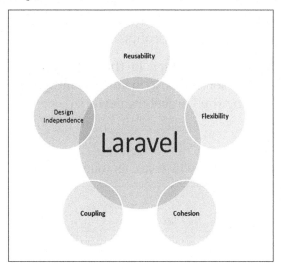

Figure 2.2: *Design Principles*

MVC in Laravel

The MVC architecture design pattern in Laravel has many advantages to application developers, architects, as well as the end users of the application.

Key Features

The following are the key features of MVC in Laravel:

- SEO Friendly
- Test Driven Development
- Maintainability and Extensibility
- Simultaneous Development

SEO Friendly

The MVC architecture pattern, along with caching, page loading, server-side rendering, and HTML metadata, makes the application optimized for SEO. SEO, which stands for Search Engine Optimization, makes the site optimized for search engines and improves the website traffic.

Importance of SEO

In developing a website, the driving factor to make a profit is directly proportional to the number of visitors on the website. Search Engine Optimization (SEO) is critical to the success of a web application/website as SEO makes it more visible to a greater number of users. This means that more traffic will be directed to the website, leading to higher potential profits.

Having the MVC architecture pattern in the application gives the advantage of SEO capabilities. This serves as a major advantage to the clients whose applications are built using the Laravel framework.

Principles

SEO is based on five principles, which are as follows (see *Figure* 2.3):

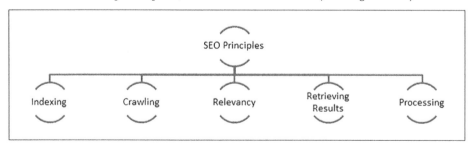

Figure 2.3: *SEO Principles*

- **Indexing**: The fetched results are indexed and stored in the database. The index helps uniquely identify the result fetched.

- **Crawling**: The crawler (software) scrapes the web to fetch all the results. This process is called crawling. In the case of Google, it is called Googlebot.

- **Relevancy**: The is a possibility of correlation between the different fetched results. The search engine measures the relevancy of the fetched web page to the index.

- **Retrieving Results:** The crucial step in SEO is to retrieve the results, that is, retrieving the best-matched results.

- **Processing**: Processing is a core SEO principle. It refers to the comparison between the search query and the result string. This comparison is performed with the indexes of data in the database

Test Driven Development

The MVC architecture pattern supports Test Driven Development (TDD).

Having the TDD helps bring a more traditional innovation to building Laravel applications and reduces the time required to develop applications with testing.

Simultaneous Development

The logical separation of operations in the application gives the power to develop the components separately. This means the application components can be broken down into logically separate components, which can be simultaneously developed, leading to a quick turnaround time for the application development.

Simultaneous Development also allows us to build features quickly and independently and then combine them using MVC principles. This ensures faster delivery of software and also makes it easier to incorporate new features and improve on the existing features.

Maintainability and Extensibility

The MVC architecture enables the application to be easy to maintain. Once an application is developed and used by users – many new insights might be discovered. It is important to incorporate these insights into the applications. It is also possible that the original team of developers who worked on the application have moved to a new project. In this case, a new team of developers will work on maintaining the application. With the MVC architecture pattern in development, the logical separation of responsibilities makes it better and easier for someone new to understand the code, making the code maintainable.

The current application can be added with additional features, and this is achieved by the MVC pattern principles. The MVC architecture makes code to be easily extendable with new capabilities. This adds to the maintainability feature of MVC.

Models in Laravel

The Model component in Laravel interacts with the database layer and the controller layer. It is also called the Data Logic component in the MVC architecture pattern.

The role of the Model component is to fetch and retrieve data from the database, as well as query the database for the desired data. In interacting with the database layer, all the CRUD (Create, Read, Update, Delete) operations are handled by the Model component. The Model components fetch the logic of the various operations from the Controller layer and are responsible for all the executions of operations, storing the result of the operations, and managing the changes in the data within the database.

The Model component interacts with the Controller layer and informs the Model component about the data flow in the application. It takes full ownership of the data flow in the application, from the UI to the database, with the Controller component serving as the intermediary.

Views in Laravel

The Views component in Laravel comprises all the components that are visible to the end-user on the application. The end user interacts with the application through the User Interface (UI), and the UI components, such as input boxes and buttons, are all encompassed within the View components in the MVC architectural pattern.

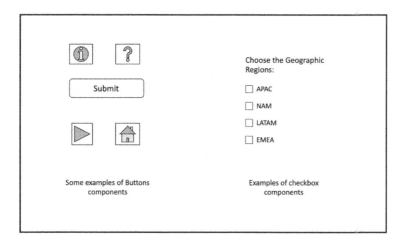

Figure 2.4: *View Component in Laravel*

Figure 2.4 displays the various examples of the View components. To summarize the View Components, it encompasses all the components and elements that are visible to the user when he/she interacts with the application interface.

Controllers in Laravel

The Controller component in the Laravel MVC architecture is the **Brain** of the application. The Controller is responsible for managing how the data in the application is controlled and also interacts with the Model and View components to decide how the data is displayed in the application. Controller components are also responsible for performing the operations that the user performs via the user interface of the application. This can be any CRUD (Create, Read, Update, Delete) operation or any feature programmed in the application. All these are the responsibilities of the Controller component.

Conclusion

In this chapter, we examined the key concept that makes building and maintaining applications in Laravel seamless. We delved into the MVC architectural pattern, exploring its history and the need for such an architectural pattern. This chapter focused on the MVC architecture pattern and how it is powerful and makes Laravel powerful.

Next, we explored the MVC pattern in depth, examining the responsibilities of each of the components along with the design principles that govern the architectural pattern. These design patterns serve as a critical benefit in using the MVC architecture pattern and also enable the programmer to use these design patterns to the fullest.

Then, we looked at the MVC architecture pattern in Laravel. We discussed key features, namely, SEO Friendly, Test Driven Development (TDD), Maintainability and Extensibility, and Simultaneous Development. These key features help in making our applications easily adopted in the industry and provide advanced modern features like SEO, which make the application scalable.

Additionally, we examined Models, Views, and Controllers in Laravel, understanding how to create these components in application development and utilizing them to stay true to the design principles and adapt the key features in the application.

The MVC architecture pattern is like the backbone of Laravel, and this chapter provides all the information, focusing on features, principles, and MVC in the context of Laravel.

In the next chapter, we will explore Routers and Views in Laravel.

## CHAPTER 3

Routers and Views in Laravel

Introduction

This chapter covers the routers and views in Laravel, which are an essential part of web development. The chapter will start with the basics and lead up to complex topics relating to routers and views. The chapter will also discuss the different types of routers and views in Laravel and how to create these components.

Structure

In this chapter, the focus will be on the following topics:

- Routers in Laravel
  - Introduction to routers
  - Routes directory
  - Router methods
  - Types of routers
  - Optional parameters
  - Regular expression constraints
  - Route groups
  - Cross-origin resource sharing
  - Caching

- Views in Laravel
    - o Creating views
    - o Views and view Extensions
    - o Data and views
    - o View composers and creators
    - o View optimization

Routers in Laravel

While developing the Laravel web application, it is important to have a programmatic way to route or provide a way to access the application's capabilities. This is where we need 'Routers in our application.

Introduction to Routers

Routers are the URLs that an end user uses in order to interact with different features of the web application. It is the endpoint that is accessed by the user to fetch and transmit data in and out of the web application.

The fundamental syntax to understand routing is as follows:

```
use Illuminate\Support\Facades\Route;


Route::get('/welcome, function () {


    return 'Hello Reader';


});
```

The following is the snapshot of the output on the browser:

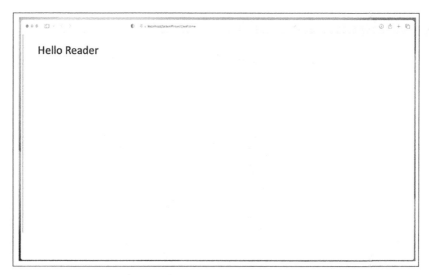

Figure 3.1: *Router Welcome Example*

Routes Directory

Your route files, which can be found in the **routes** directory, include definitions for all Laravel routes.

The **AppProvidersRouteServiceProvider** in your application will automatically load these files. Routes for your web interface are defined in the **routes/web.php** file. These routes fall within the purview of the web middleware group, which offers capabilities like CSRF protection and session state. The **api** middleware group is applied to the stateless routes in **routes/api.php**.

You must begin by defining routes in your **routes/web.php** file for the majority of applications. By typing the defined route's URL into your browser, you can access the routes defined in **routes/web.php**.

Let's look at an example. To access the following route, you can navigate to http://example.com/ep1 in your browser.

```
use App\Http\Controllers\UserController;


Route::get('/ep1, [UserController::class, 'index']);
```

Router Methods

The router enables a programmer to register routes that respond to any HTTP verb.

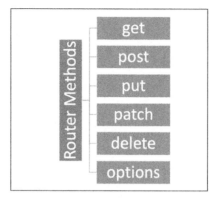

Figure 3.2: *Router Methods*

The get, post, put, patch, delete, and options methods should be defined before the any, match, and redirect methods when building multiple routes that share the same URI. This means that the appropriate route is matched to the incoming request.

Types of Routers

There are four main types of routers which are extensively used in Laravel:

- Redirect routes
- View routes
- Route list
- Fallback routes

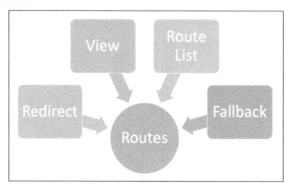

Figure 3.3: *Router Types*

Redirect Routes

The **Route::redirect** method can be used to define a route that redirects to another URI. With the help of this approach, you can quickly do a straightforward redirect without having to construct a whole route or controller:

```
Route::redirect('/ep1', '/ep2');
```

The status code can be customized as well for the route:

```
Route::redirect('/ep1', '/ep2', 301);
```

Alternatively, the **Route::permanentRedirect** method can be used to get a 301 status code:

```
Route::permanentRedirect('/ep1', '/ep2');
```

View Routes

Use the **Route::view** method if your route needs to return only a **view**. This technique offers a shortcut so that you do not need to define a whole route or controller, similar to the redirect method.

The view method takes two arguments:

a URI as the first and

a view name as the second.

As an optional third argument, you may also supply an array of data to the view:

```
Route::view('/about', 'about');
```

```
Route::view('/about', 'about', ['state' => 'Reader']);
```

The Route List

The **route:list** The artisan command can quickly give you a summary of all the routes that your application has created.

You can tell Laravel to show the route middleware by adding the -v option to the command: By default, the route middleware that is assigned to each route will not be displayed in the **route:list** output.

```
php artisan route:list -v
```

By adding the **--except-vendor** option while running the **route:list**, you can also instruct Laravel to conceal any routes.

```
php artisan route:list --except-vendor
```

Likewise, by specifying the --only-vendor option when executing the route, you may tell Laravel to only display routes that are created by third-party packages.

```
php artisan route:list --only-vendor
```

Fallback Routes

You can provide a route that will be followed if no other route fits the incoming request by using the **Route::fallback** function. Unhandled requests typically result in your application's exception handler rendering a "404" page. However, all middleware in the **web** middleware group will apply to the route as the **fallback** route is normally defined in your **routes/web.php** file. You are allowed to supplement this route with other middleware as necessary:

```
Route::fallback(function () {

    // Code Logic

});
```

Route Parameters

Route parameters must always be enclosed in braces and should only contain letters of the alphabet. Within the names of route parameters, underscores (_) are also permitted.

The order in which the route callbacks and controller arguments are passed determines how the route parameters are injected; the arguments' names are irrelevant.

List your route parameters after your dependencies if you want the Laravel service container to automatically:

```
use Illuminate\Http\Request;


Route::get('/user/{num}', function (Request $request, string $num) {

    return 'User '.$num;

});
```

Optional Parameters

Sometimes a route parameter that isn't always in the URI needs to be specified. Put a question mark (?) after the parameter name to do this. Make sure to assign a default value to the respective route variable:

```
Route::get('/user/{place?}', function (string $place = null) {

    return $place;

});


Route::get('/user/{place?}', function (string $place = 'London') {

    return $place;

});
```

Regular Expressions Constraints

Using the `where` method on a route object, you can restrict the format of your route arguments. The `where` method accepts a regular expression that specifies how the parameter should be constrained in addition to the parameter's name.

Note: Let's understand regular expressions before diving deep into the Regular expressions constraints.

Regular Expressions

Regex is short for regular expression. A string of various characters known as a regex, regexp, or regular expression describes a specific search pattern. Additionally, it is referred to or called a rational expression.

It is mostly utilized for text string manipulation and search. Simply said, regular expressions make it straightforward to look for patterns and replace them with those that match.

`*`

It is used to match strings with no restriction or rule. Generally used in combination with other rules.

`{}`

The number of times the previous regular expression should be applied is indicated by the integer values wrapped in.

`<^> or <$> or <[ A-Z]>`

These expressions among others help in finding the length of string. The first two regex matches the entire subject string and the last one matches any single uppercase character from A to Z.

`^[a-zA-Z]`

It is used to match strings that either begin with a small- or capital-letter character.

`[0-9]`

It is used to match a digit from 0 to 9.

`[aeiou]`

Only the lower-case vowels are matched by this square bracket.

`[AEIOU]`

Only the upper-case vowels are matched by this square bracket.

`ab[^3-7]`

It matches any numbers or characters that don't have definitions inside the square bracket.

`(  )`

It is employed to match everything included in the simple bracket.

`{   }`

It is employed to match everything included in the curly bracket.

`[    ]`

It is employed to match everything included in the square bracket.

Regular Expressions Constraints

```
Route::get('/user/{name}', function (string $name) {

    // Code Logic

})->where('name', '[A-Za-z]+');


Route::get('/user/{id}', function (string $id) {

    // Code Logic

})->where('id', '[0-9]+');


Route::get('/user/{id}/{name}', function (string $id, string $name) {

    // Code Logic

})->where(['id' => '[0-9]+', 'name' => '[a-z]+']);
```

There are a number of helper methods as well:

```
Route::get('/user/{id}/{name}', function (string $id, string $name) {

    // Code Logic

})->whereNumber('id')->whereAlpha('name');
```

```
Route::get('/user/{name}', function (string $name) {

    // Code Logic

})->whereAlphaNumeric('name');



Route::get('/user/{id}', function (string $id) {

    // Code Logic

})->whereUuid('id');



Route::get('/user/{id}', function (string $id) {

    // Code Logic

})->whereUlid('id');



Route::get('/category/{category}', function (string $category) {

    // Code Logic

})->whereIn('category', ['movie', 'song', 'painting']);
```

A 404 HTTP response will be given if the inbound request does not comply with the route pattern limitations.

Route Groups

Route groups are a core concept of developing Laravel Applications. Route groups enable and provide the feature to share route attributes, including middleware across numerous routes. This also enables us to avoid describing the qualities of each individual route.

With the built-in intelligent capabilities, the nested groups are capable of compressing and merge different attributes present in the parent group. This process is achieved as follows:

1.   The where conditions are merged.

2.   The Middleware is merged.

3.   Names are appended.

4.   Prefixes are appended.

As required, the namespace delimiters and slashes are automatically inserted into URI prefixes.

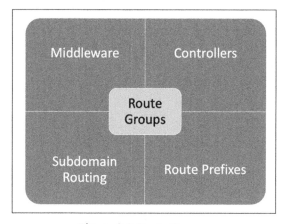

Figure 3.4: *Route Groups*

Middleware

You can use the middleware method before declaring the group to assign middleware to each route within it. The middleware is executed in the array in the following order:

```
Route::middleware(['m1', 'm2'])->group(function () {
    Route::get('/', function () {


        // Uses m1 & m2 middleware
```

```
// Code Logic

    });

    Route::get('/city/pollution', function () {

        // Uses m1 & m2 middleware

// Code Logic

    });

    Route::get('/city/waterSupply', function () {

        // Uses m1 & m2 middleware

            // Code Logic

    });
});
```

Controllers

If a group of routes all use the same controller, you can define the shared controller for the group's routes using the controller method. The controller method that they call can therefore be provided when defining the routes:

```
use App\Http\Controllers\CityController;

Route::controller(CityController::class)->group(function () {

    Route::get('/city/{id}', 'show');
```

```
    Route::post('/city', 'location');

});
```

Additional ways to define routes

In the scenario of a single invokable method in the controller, use as following:

```
    Route::post('/file', FileHandler::class)
```

Additionally, the resource controller can be pointed to as:

```
    Route::resource('users', UserController::class)
```

Subdomain Routing

For instances when you need to capture a part of the subdomain to use in a route or controller, the subdomain routing feature of Laravel is useful. Subdomain routing can be managed using 'Route Groups'. The subdomain routes can make use of the parameters same as the route parameters and allow the use of the functionality to achieve the results using subdomain routing. Before defining the group, the `domain` method may be called to specify the subdomain:

```
Route::domain('{city}.example.com')->group(function () {

    Route::get('city/{id}', function (string $name, string $id) {

        // Code Logic

    });
});
```

Route Prefixes

Each route in the group may be prefixed with a specific URI using the `prefix` method. For instance, you might wish to append **admin:** to the beginning of every route URI in the group.

```
Route::prefix('hr')->group(function () {

    Route::get('/employees', function () {

        // Matches The "/hr/employees" URL

    });

});
```

In order to prefix each route in the group, which also has a valid URL – the Laravel in-built method can be used. The method **prefix** helps achieve this functionality. A good practice is to make use of **admin** and prefix the group with the same.

We will make sure to include the trailing because the given string is prefixed to the route name exactly as it is specified. An element of the prefix:

```
Route::name('admin.')->group(function () {
    Route::get('/city', function () {

        // Route assigned name "admin.city"

    })->name('city');
});
```

Cross-origin Resource Sharing (CORS)

With values that you specify, Laravel may automatically reply to CORS **OPTIONS** HTTP requests. You may configure every CORS setting in the **config/cors.php** configuration file for your application.

The **HandleCors** middleware, which comes preinstalled in your global middleware stack, will automatically handle the **OPTIONS** requests. The HTTP kernel (**App\ Http\Kernel**) of your application houses the whole global middleware stack.

Caching

Use Laravel's route cache when releasing your application to the live internet. It will take much less time to register all of your application's routes if you use the route cache. Run the **route:cache** Artisan command to generate a route cache.

```
php artisan route:cache
```

Your cached routes file will be loaded on each request once you run this command. Keep in mind that you must create a new route cache if you add any new routes. As a result, you should only execute the **route:cache** command during the deployment of your project.

You could take the route cache, and use the clear command:

```
php artisan route:clear
```

Views in Laravel

Views offer a practical method for organizing all of our HTML into different files.

The html code needed by your application is contained in views, a Laravel technique that separates the presentation logic from the controller logic and domain logic. Resources/views are the path of the views folder, where they can be found.

The resources/views directory houses views, which separate your controller/ application code from your presentation logic. The Blade templating language is typically used when using Laravel to create view templates. A straightforward view might resemble this:

```
<!-- View stored in resources/views/welcome.blade.php -->

<html>

    <body>

        <h2>Hello, {{ $name }}</h2>
```

```
    </body>

</html>

To return the view:

Route::get('/', function () {

    return view('welcome', ['name' => 'ABC']);

});
```

Creating Views

By adding a file with the **.blade.php** extension to the **resources/views** directory of your application, you can build a view. The framework is informed that a Blade template is present in the file by the **.blade.php** extension. Blade templates include HTML and Blade directives that make it simple to iterate through data, echo values, and generate "if" statements.

Using the global **view** helper, you can return a view you've constructed from one of your application's routes or controllers:

```
Route::get('/', function () {

    return view('welcome', ['name' => 'ABC']);

});
```

The **View** facade can also be used to return views:

```
use Illuminate\Support\Facades\View;

return View::make('welcome', ['name' => 'ABC']);
```

As evident in the preceding code, the name of the view file in the **resources/views** directory corresponds to the first argument supplied to the **view** helper.

An array of data that ought to be made available to the view is the second argument. In this instance, we are passing the **name** variable, which is written in Blade syntax and displayed on the view.

Views and View Extensions

The views can be defined in different forms. Let's look at the views and the extension of the view feature.

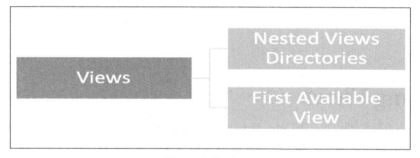

Figure 3.5: *Views*

Nested Views Directories

The **resources/views** directory's subdirectories are another place where views can be nested. Nested views may be referred to using "dot" notation.

For instance, if your view is located at **resources/views/admin/welcome.blade.php**, you could return it using the following syntax from a route or controller in your application:

```
return view('admin.welcome', $data);
```

The . character shouldn't be used in view directory names.

First Available View

You can build the first view in an array of views by using the **first** method of the **View** facade. If your application or package permits views to be modified or replaced, this might be helpful:

```
use Illuminate\Support\Facades\View;
```

```
return View::first(['custom.playground', 'playground'], $data);
```

Use the **View** facade to check whether a view is available. If the view is present, the **exists** method will return **true**.

```
use Illuminate\Support\Facades\View;
```

```
if (View::exists('emails.employee')) {

    // Code Logic

}
```

Data and Views

The data to be given in this way should be an array containing key/value pairs. You can use the data's keys, such as `<?php echo $name;?>`, to retrieve each value in your view after delivering the data to it.

You can add certain pieces of data to the view using the **with** method rather than sending the **view** helper function a whole array of data.

Before returning the view, the **with** method returns an instance of the view object so that you can chain additional methods:

```
return view('welcome')

        ->with('name', 'ABC')

        ->with('organization', 'ORGNAME');
```

Sharing Data

On rare occasions, you might need to share data with every view your application renders. Use the **share** method of the **View** facade to accomplish this. The **share** method should typically be called from a service provider's **boot** method. You can construct a different service provider to house them or add them to the **App\ Providers\AppServiceProvider** class. And it is mandatory to register it in the **config/app.php** in order for it to work.

```php
<?php


namespace App\Providers;


use Illuminate\Support\Facades\View;


class AppServiceProvider extends ServiceProvider
{

    /**
     * Register any application services.
     */

    public function register(): void
    {

        // Code Logic

    }

    /**
     * Bootstrap any application services.
     */

    public function boot(): void
    {
```

```
        View::share('key', 'value');


    }
}
```

View Composers and Creators

The View composers and creators have fundamental differences in the way it enables robustness to code.

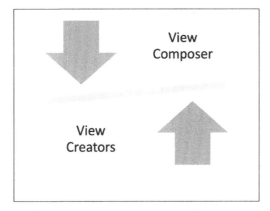

Figure 3.6: *View Composers and Creators*

View Composers

When a view is rendered, callbacks or class methods called view composers are invoked. A view composer can assist you in centralizing your logic if you have data that needs to be tied to a view each time it is rendered. If the same view is returned by many routes or controllers in your application and requires the same set of data, view composers may prove to be especially helpful.

View composers will often be registered with one of the service providers for your application. For this example, we'll suppose that a new **App\Providers\ViewServiceProvider** has been built to contain this functionality.

To register the view composer, we'll use the **composer** method of the **View** facade. You are free to arrange class-based view composers in any way you see fit since Laravel does not provide a default directory for them.

To store all of your application's view composers, for instance, you may make an **app/View/Composers** directory:

```php
<?php

namespace App\Providers;

use App\View\Composers\ProfileComposer;
use Illuminate\Support\Facades;
use Illuminate\Support\ServiceProvider;
use Illuminate\View\View;

class ViewServiceProvider extends ServiceProvider
{
    /**
     * Register any application services.
     */

    public function register(): void
    {

        // Code Logic

    }

    /**
     * Bootstrap any application services.
     */

    public function boot(): void
    {
        // Using class based composers
```

```
        Facades\View::composer('profile', ProfileComposer::class);

        // Using closure based composers

        Facades\View::composer('cityPollution', function (View $view) {

            // Code Logic

        });

        Facades\View::composer('introduction', function (View $view) {

            // Code Logic

        });
    }
}
```

The **compose** method of the **App\View\Composers\ProfileComposer** class now that the composer has been registered will be called.

```
<?php

namespace App\View\Composers;

use App\Repositories\UserRepository;
use Illuminate\View\View;

class ProfileComposer
{
    /**
     * Create a new profile composer.
     */
```

```
public function __construct(

    protected CityRepository $city,

) {}

/**
 * Bind data to the view.
 */

public function compose(View $view): void
{

    $view->with('count', $this->city->count());

}
}
```

As you can see, the *service container* resolves all view composers, allowing you to type-hint any dependencies you require inside a composer's constructor.

Multiple Views with Composer

By giving the composer method an array of views as the first argument, you can attach a view composer to several views at once:

```
use App\Views\Composers\MultiComposer;
use Illuminate\Support\Facades\View;

View::composer(

    ['welcome', 'dashboard'],
    MultiComposer::class
```

```
);
```

The * character is also accepted by the composer method as a wildcard, enabling you to add a composer to all views:

```
use Illuminate\Support\Facades;
use Illuminate\View\View;


Facades\View::composer('*', function (View $view) {

    // Code Logic

});
```

View Creators

Similar to view composers, view creators are executed as soon as the view is instantiated rather than waiting until the view is about to render. Use the **creator** method to register a view creator:

```
use App\View\Creators\ProfileCreator;
use Illuminate\Support\Facades\View;


View::creator('profile', ProfileCreator::class);
```

The preceding code makes use of the **creator** method and registers a view creator.

View Optimization

Blade template views are by default compiled as needed. If a view is rendered by a request, Laravel will check to see if a compiled version of the view is available.

In the event that the file is present, Laravel will ascertain whether the uncompiled view has undergone more recent changes than the compiled view. Laravel will recompile the view if the compiled view is either missing or the uncompiled view has been altered.

Due to a potential slight performance hit from compiling views during the request, Laravel offers the **view:cache** Precompile all the views that your application uses with an artisan task.

You might want to execute this command as part of your deployment procedure for improved performance:

```
php artisan view:cache
```

To clear the view cache:

```
php artisan view:clear
```

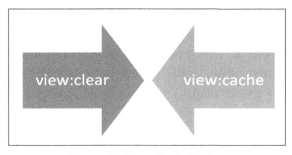

Figure 3.7: *View Optimization*

Conclusion

Routers and views, two crucial components of web development, are the focus of this chapter of the book. At the beginning of the chapter, we covered the importance of routers and views in online applications as well as how Laravel makes use of both. There are several topics covered, including routers and views and their various types, strategies, and configurations.

An overview of Laravel routers, the URLs that users used to access various web application capabilities, is provided at the beginning of the chapter. Then, we saw the basic syntax example for routing and explored how routers are used to fetch and transmit data into and out of the application.

The next chapter will focus on building Controllers and Blade templates in Laravel. It will explain the importance of controllers and Blade in web development and how they are used in Laravel.

Points to Remember

- The chapter explores the route files that define all Laravel routes, which are located in the routes directory. It describes the function of the `App\ Providers\RouteServiceProvider` and how the route files are loaded automatically. It emphasizes that web interface routes, which offer features like CSRF protection and session state, are created in the `routes/web.php` file and belong to the web middleware group. The `routes/api.php` file defines stateless routes for the API, which are a part of the `api` middleware group.

- Then, the chapter explores router methods, which let programmers register routes that react to different HTTP verbs. When creating several routes with the same URI, it lists a number of common router methods and stresses the order in which they should be declared.

- The View section opens with an introduction to Laravel views and a discussion of how they help to render a web page's HTML representation. It highlights how views enable developers to segregate the display logic from the business logic of the application, resulting in simpler and more readable code.

- The first subject discussed in this part is creating views. Views in Laravel are, by default, kept in the resources/views directory. It covers how to reference views in routes and controllers and goes through the process of generating a view file.

- The chapter then examines the various view types that Laravel offers. The default templating engine in Laravel, Blade Views, is discussed. It offers capabilities like conditional statements and loops, and includes reusable code snippets.

- For developers who favor working with plain PHP code, the chapter also highlights the availability of plain PHP views. How to send data from controllers to views is covered in the section on data and views. It explains how to provide data to views using the method and the compact function, enabling developers to display dynamic content based on the supplied data.

- Then, as a means of transferring data across different views or carrying out operations on them, view composers and creators are provided. View composers are callbacks that are executed when particular views are produced, allowing data to be shared with those views. View creators, on the other hand, let programmers take action before a view is produced.

## CHAPTER 4

Building Controllers and Blade Templates

Introduction

This chapter covers Controllers and Blade in Laravel, which are crucial components in web development. It will explain the importance of Controllers and Blade in web development and how they are used in Laravel. The chapter will also discuss how to use Controllers with views, redirects, directives, and Blade as template engines.

Structure

In this chapter, we will discuss the following topics:

- Controllers with Views in Laravel
  - Controllers
  - Resource Controllers
  - Constructor Injection
  - Method Injection
- Redirects in Laravel
  - Redirect Helper
  - Redirecting to Named Routes
  - Redirecting to Controller Actions
- Directives in Laravel
  - Conditional Directive
  - Switch Directive

   o   Auth Directive
   o   Loops
   o   Once Directive
- Blade as Template Engines in Laravel
   o   Data in Blade
   o   HTML Entity Encoding
   o   Components
      ▪   Rendering Components
      ▪   Passing Data
   o   Layouts
   o   Rendering Blade Templates
   o   Rendering Blade Fragments

Controllers with Views in Laravel

Controllers in the MVC architecture are simply classes that group the functionality of one or more routes together. Particularly, if your application is organized in a traditionally CRUD-like fashion, controllers prefer to group related routes together.

A good coding and application development practice is to separate the application logic as per the Model-View-Controller (MVC) logic. It may feel easier to have all logic in the controller, but that will drive away from the purpose and the intention of the MVC architecture.

A controller may manage all the actions that can be performed on a specific resource, such as:

CRUD – Create, Read, Update, Delete

Controllers

The `make:controller` Artisan command is used to rapidly create a new controller, and the `app/Http/Controllers` directory is where the Laravel application's controllers are kept by default.

For example:

```
php artisan make:controller UserController
```

Using the controller syntax, let's look at the following example to create a controller in Laravel:

```php
<?php

namespace App\Http\Controllers;

use App\Models\User;
use Illuminate\View\View;

class UserController extends Controller
{
    /*
     * Display the details for a given user.
     */
    public function show(string $id): View
    {
        return view('user.details', [
            'user' => User::findOrFail($id)
        ]);
    }
}
```

The display function on the `App\Http\Controllers\UserController` class is called and the route parameters are provided to it when an incoming request matches the specified route URI.

Resource Controllers

It is customary to execute the same sets of actions against each resource in your application, especially if you consider each Eloquent model to be a **resource** rather than a data object. Consider a scenario in which your application includes both a `Painting` model and a `Museum` model. Users most likely have the ability to add, read, modify, or remove these resources.

Due to this common use scenario, Laravel resource routing only requires one line of code to assign the normal create, read, update, and delete (CRUD) routes to a controller. We can utilize the **make:controller** to get going here. Use the **--resource** argument of the controller Artisan command to rapidly construct a controller to handle these actions:

```
php artisan make:controller PaintingController --resource
```

The controller created by this command will be located in **app/Http/Controllers/PaintingController.php**. For each of the possible resource operations, a method will be present in the controller. Following that, you can set up a resource route that directs traffic to the controller:

```
use App\Http\Controllers\PaintingController;

Route::resource(paintings, PaintingController::class);
```

Multiple routes are created by this single route declaration to handle various operations on the resource. Each of these actions will already have methods stubbed in the created controller. Remember that the **route:list** Artisan command may always be used to receive a quick overview of the routes in your application.

Additionally, by providing an array to the **resources** methods, you may even register many resource controllers at once:

```
Route::resources([
    'paintings' => PaintingController::class,
    'picture' => PictureController::class,
]);
```

Verb	URI	Action	Route Name
GET	/paintings	index	paintings.index
GET	/paintings/create	create	paintings.create

POST	/paintings	store	paintings.store
GET	/paintings/{paintings}	show	paintings.show
GET	/paintings/ {paintings}/edit	edit	paintings.edit
PUT/PATCH	/paintings/{paintings}	update	paintings. update
DELETE	/paintings/{paintings}	destroy	paintings. destroy

Table 4.1: *Action, Routes, and URLs*

Constructor Injection

All Laravel controllers are resolved using the Laravel service container. You may type-hint any dependencies your controller might require in its constructor as a consequence. Automatic resolution and injection of the given dependencies into the controller instance will take place:

```php
<?php

namespace App\Http\Controllers;

use App\Repositories\EmployeeRepository;

class EmployeeController extends Controller
{
    /*
     * Create a new controller instance.
     */
    public function __construct(
        protected EmployeeRepository $employees,
    ) {}
}
```

Method Injection

You may type-hint dependencies on the methods of your controller in addition to injecting requirements in constructors. Injecting the **Illuminate\Http\Request** object into your controller functions is a typical application of method injection:

```php
<?php

namespace App\Http\Controllers;

use Illuminate\Http\RedirectResponse;
use Illuminate\Http\Request;

class EmployeeController extends Controller
{

    // Store a new employee.

    public function store(Request $request): RedirectResponse
    {
        $name = $request->name;

        // Store the employee...

        return redirect('/employees');
    }
}
```

List your route arguments after your other requirements if your controller function additionally requires input from a route parameter. For instance, if your route is specified as follows:

```php
use App\Http\Controllers\EmployeeController;
```

```
Route::put('/employee/{id}', [EmployeeController::class, 'update']);
```

Redirects in Laravel

Redirect responses are derived from the **Illuminate\Http\RedirectResponse** class and include the appropriate headers for sending the user to a different URL.

Redirect Helper

The easiest way to create a redirect in Laravel is using the Redirect Helper. Let's look at an example of creating a redirect in Laravel:

```
Route::get('/aboutMe', function () {
    return redirect('/home/aboutMe');
});
```

In some circumstances, such as when incorrect or incomplete information is submitted, you might want to send the user back to the previous webpage. Use the global **back** helper function to do this. Make sure the route using the **back** function is using the web middleware group or has all of the session middleware applied because this functionality uses the session:

```
Route::post('/user/aboutMe', function () {

    // Validate the request

    return back()->withInput();

});
```

Redirecting to Named Routes

An instance of **Illuminate\Routing\Redirector** is returned when the **redirect** helper in a Laravel application is used without any arguments, enabling you to call any method on the **Redirector** instance. For instance, you can use the **route** method to create a **RedirectResponse** to a specific route:

```
return redirect()->route('register');
```

To add parameters to pass it as a second argument to the **route** method:

```
// For a route with URI: dashboard/{id}

return redirect()->route('dashboard', ['id' => 1]);
```

Laravel also offers a global **to_route** function that can be used to redirect and route.

Redirecting to Controller Actions

In Laravel, redirects to controller operations are also possible. To achieve this, provide the **action** method with the controller and action name:

```
use App\Http\Controllers\EmployeeController;

return redirect()->action([EmployeeController::class, 'taxID']);
```

You can add arguments as the second argument to the **action** method if your controller route calls for them:

```
return redirect()->action(
    [EmployeeController::class, 'dashboard'], ['id' => 1]
);
```

Redirecting - Flashed Session Data

Normally, flashing data to the session and redirecting to a new URL happen simultaneously. Usually, you flash a success message to the session after completing an activity successfully. In a single, fluid method chain, you may build a **RedirectResponse** object and flash data to the session for convenience:

```
Route::post('/employee/profile', function () {

    // Update the employee's profile

    return redirect('/dashboard')->with('status', 'Employee Profile Data
updated!');
});
```

Before sending the user to a different page, you may flash the input data from the current request to the session using the **withInput** method offered by the **RedirectResponse** class. Whenever you make the following request, you may quickly recover the input after it has been flashed to the session:

```
    return back()->withInput();
```

You can show the session's flashing message when the user is redirected. As an illustration, using Blade syntax:

```
@if (session('status'))
    <div class="alert alert-success">
        {{ session('status') }}
    </div>
@endif
```

Directives in Laravel

Directives are explicit instructions that may be used within Blade templates in Laravel to carry out certain logic or actions. The Templating Engine for Laravel, known as Blade, enables you to create expressive, tidy, and readable views for your application.

In Laravel, directives are identified by the symbol **@** and the directive name. They offer a quick and stylish method of running PHP code inside of your Blade templates without clogging the display with PHP tags.

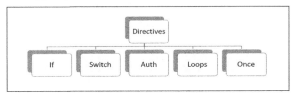

Figure 4.1: Type of Directives in Laravel

Conditional Directives

The if directives are used to specify conditions in the logic building of the Laravel application. The following are the different directives, as shown in *Figure 4.2*:

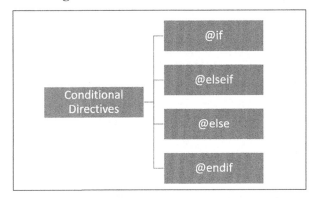

Figure 4.2: Conditional Directives in Laravel

The directives **@if**, **@elseif**, **@else**, and **@endif** can be used to create if statements. These directives perform the same tasks as their PHP equivalents:

```
@if (count($fruits) === 1)
    There is one fruit!
@elseif (count($records) > 1)
    There are multiple fruits.
@else
    There are no fruits.
@endif
```

The **@isset** and **@empty** directives can be used as practical substitutes for their respective PHP functions in addition to the conditional directives already covered:

```
@isset($fruits)
    // $fruits is defined and is not null
@endisset


@empty($fruits)
    // $fruits is "empty"
@endempty
```

Custom if Statements

When creating basic, custom conditional statements, programming a custom directive might often be more difficult than necessary. In order to easily build unique conditional directives using closures, Blade offers the `Blade::if` function.

Switch Directive

The switch directive is an essential component in writing the logic and handling of different scenarios in Laravel.

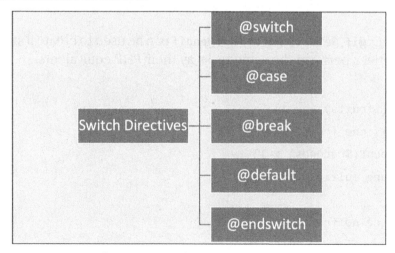

Figure 4.3: *Switch Directive in Laravel*

Let's look at using the switch directive in the code:

```
@switch($i)
    @case(1)
        Case 1
        @break

    @case(2)
        Case 2
        @break

    @default
        Default case
@endswitch
```

Auth Directive

The auth directive is useful to maintain authentication and security in application code.

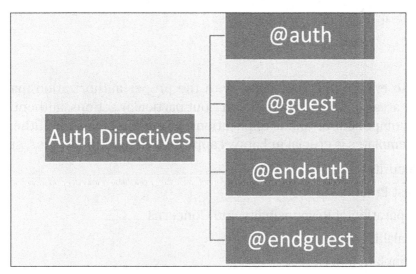

Figure 4.4: *Auth Directives in Laravel*

To easily detect whether the current user is authenticated or a guest, use the **@ auth** and **@guest** directives:

```
@auth
    // The user is authenticated
@endauth

@guest
    // The user is not authenticated
@endguest
```

The **@auth** and **@guest** directives allow you to define the authentication guard that should be verified if necessary:

```
@auth('admin')
    // The user is authenticated
@endauth

@guest('admin')
    // The user is not authenticated
@endguest
```

In order to ensure that only users with the proper authorization may access particular areas of the program or carry out particular actions, authentication is a crucial component of online applications. Using directives for authentication in Blade templates is crucial in Laravel apps for a number of reasons, such as:

- Security
- Best Practices
- Separation of Responsibility and Concerns
- Scalability
- Template Inheritance

Security, code structure, and maintainability all depend on the use of directives for authentication in Laravel apps. It encourages best practices and supports developers' effective management of the frontend views' authentication-related code.

Loops

Blade offers straightforward directives in addition to conditional statements for interacting with PHP's loop structures.

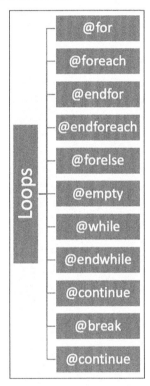

Figure 4.5: *Loop Directives in Laravel*

Again, each of these directives does the same tasks as their PHP equivalents:

```
@for ($i = 0; $i < 10; $i++)
    The current value of i is {{ $i }}
@endfor

@foreach ($employees as $employee)
    <p>This is employee {{ $employee->id }}</p>
@endforeach
```

```
@forelse ($employees as $employee)
    <li>{{ $employee->name }}</li>
@empty
    <p>No employees</p>
@endforelse

@while (true)
    <p>Forever Loop</p>
@endwhile
```

Using the **@continue** and **@break** directives, you can also use loops to skip the current iteration or break the loop:

```
@foreach ($employees as $employee)
    @if ($employee->type == 1)
        @continue
    @endif

    <li>{{ $employee->name }}</li>

    @if ($employee->number == 5)
        @break
    @endif
@endforeach
```

The continuation or break condition may also be included in the directive declaration:

```
@foreach ($employees as $employee)
    @continue($employee->type == 1)

    <li>{{ $employee->name }}</li>
```

```
        @break($employee->number == 5)
@endforeach
```

Once Directive

You may provide a section of the template that will only be evaluated once during each rendering cycle using the **@once** directive. This may help leverage stacks to push a specific piece of JavaScript into the page's header.

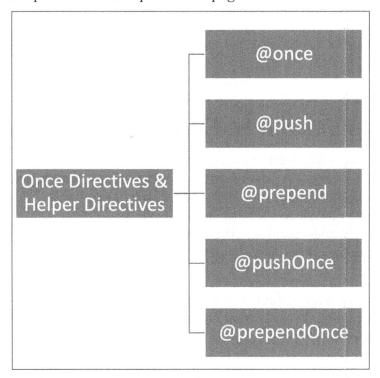

Figure 4.6: Once Directives and Helper Directives in Laravel

For instance, if you are rendering a certain component repeatedly, you might just want to push the JavaScript to the header the first time:

```
@once
    @push('scripts')
        <script>
            // Custom JavaScript script
```

```
        </script>
    @endpush
@endonce
```

The **@pushOnce** and **@prependOnce** directives are included for your convenience since the **@once** directive is frequently used in combination with the **@push** or **@ prepend** directives:

```
@pushOnce('scripts')
    <script>
        // Custom JavaScript script
    </script>
@endPushOnce
```

Blade as Template Engines in Laravel

The straightforward yet effective templating engine that comes with Laravel is called Blade. In contrast to several PHP templating engines, Blade does not prevent you from utilizing raw PHP code in your templates,. In reality, Blade adds practically no cost to your application because all templates are converted into normal PHP code and cached until they are updated. Blade template files normally reside in the **resources/views** directory and have the **.blade.php** file extension.

Using the global **view** helper, Blade views may be retrieved from routes or controllers. Additionally, data may be provided to the Blade view via the view helper's second parameter, as explained in the documentation on views:

```
Route::get('/', function () {
    return view('welcome', ['name' => 'ABC']);
});
```

Data in Blade

By enclosing the variable in curly brackets, data that is supplied to your Blade views may be shown. Consider the following route, for instance:

```
Route::get('/', function () {
    return view('welcome', ['name' => 'ABC']);
});
```

In order to display the contents inline of the variables, use double curly brackets: **{{variable_name}}**

For the preceding example, it will be:

```
Welcome, {{name}}
```

HTML Entity Encoding

Blade and Laravel helper double-encode HTML entities by default. Call the **Blade::withoutDoubleEncoding** function from your **AppServiceProvider's boot** method to stop double encoding:

```php
<?php

namespace App\Providers;

use Illuminate\Support\Facades\Blade;
use Illuminate\Support\ServiceProvider;

class AppServiceProvider extends ServiceProvider
{
    /*
     * Bootstrap any application services.
     */
    public function boot(): void
    {
        Blade::withoutDoubleEncoding();
```

```
        }
}
```

Components

Sections, layouts, and inclusions all give comparable benefits; nevertheless, some people may find the mental model of components and slots simpler to grasp. Class-based components and anonymous components are the two methods of writing components.

You may use the `make:component` Artisan command to construct a class-based component. We'll make an **Alert** component to demonstrate how to use components. The component will be placed in the **app/View/Components** directory using the `make:component` command:

```
php artisan make:component Alert
```

A view template will also be produced for the component using the `make:component` command. The **resources/views/components** directory will house the view. No further component registration is normally needed when creating components for your own application because they are immediately found in the **resources/views/components** directory and the **app/View/Components** directory:

```
php artisan make:component Forms/Input
```

The aforementioned command will place the view in the **resources/views/components/forms** directory and an **Input** component in the **app/View/Components/Forms** directory.

Use the `--view` option when using `make:controller` if you want to construct an anonymous component (a component with simply a Blade template and no class):

```
php artisan make:component forms.input --view
```

The command will create a Blade file located at the **input.blade.php** file located at **resources/views/components/forms** that can be rendered as a component via **<x-forms.input />**.

Rendering Components

You may use a Blade component tag inside one of your Blade templates to show a component. Blade component tags begin with the letter **x-** and the component class's kebab case name:

For example:

```
<x-alert/>
```

```
<x-user-profile/>
```

Use the character **.** to denote directory nesting if the component class is further nested within the **app/View/Components** directory. For instance, if we believe a component to be located in **app/View/Components/Inputs/Button.php**, we may render it as follows:

```
<x-inputs.button/>
```

You may add a **shouldRender** function to your component class to conditionally render your component. The component won't be rendered if the **shouldRender** function returns false:

```
use Illuminate\Support\Str;

/*
 * Whether the component should be rendered
 */
public function shouldRender(): bool
{
    return Str::length($this->message) > 0;
}
```

Passing Data

Using HTML properties, you may provide data to Blade components. Simple HTML attribute strings can be used to pass the component hard-coded, basic data. PHP variables and expressions must be supplied to the component using attributes with the character : in the prefix:

```
<x-alert type="error" :message="$message"/>
```

The class constructor of the component should contain a definition of each data attribute. A component's view will always have access to all public attributes on the component. It is not required to transfer the data from the **render** method of the component to the view.

```php
<?php

namespace App\View\Components;

use Illuminate\View\Component;
use Illuminate\View\View;

class Alert extends Component
{
    /*
     * Component Instance.
     */
    public function __construct(
        public string $type,
        public string $message,
    ) {}

    /*
     * Get the view / contents that represent the component.
     */
```

```
    public function render(): View
    {
        return view('components.alert');
    }
}
```

(**Source**: Laravel.com/docs)

To display the contents of the component, display the values of the variables as follows:

```
<div class="alert alert-{{ $type }}">
    {{ $message }}
</div>
```

Layouts

The majority of web applications have the same overall layout across all of their pages. If we had to duplicate the full layout HTML in each view we created, it would be tremendously time-consuming and difficult to maintain our program. We can specify this layout as a single Blade component and utilize it across the rest of our application:

```
<!-- resources/views/components/layout.blade.php -->

<html>
    <head>
        <title>{{ $title ?? 'Grocery List' }}</title>
    </head>
    <body>
        <h1>Things to Buy</h1>
        <hr/>
        {{ $item }}
    </body>
```

```
</html>
```

We can make a Blade view that makes use of the **layout** component after it has been defined.

For instance, in this illustration, we'll create a straightforward view to show our task list:

```
<!-- resources/views/product.blade.php -->
```

```
<x-layout>
    @foreach ($products as $product)
        {{ $product }}
    @endforeach
</x-layout>
```

Keep in mind that any material that is injected into a component will go into the layout component's **$item** default variable. As you may have observed, if a **$title** slot is given, our **layout** also honors it; otherwise, a default title is shown.

Template Inheritance

Additionally, **template inheritance** may be used to generate layouts. Before the advent of components, this was the main method of application development.

Let's start by looking at a straightforward example. We'll look at a page layout first. It is simple to specify this style as a single Blade view because the majority of web applications keep the same overall layout across many pages:

```
<!-- resources/views/layouts/app.blade.php -->
```

```
<html>
    <head>
        <title>App Name - @yield('title')</title>
    </head>
    <body>
```

```
    @section('sidebar')
        This is the master sidebar.
    @show

    <div class="container">
        @yield('content')
    </div>
</body>
</html>
```

This file has normal HTML markup, as you can see. However, pay attention to the **@section** and **@yield** directives. The **@yield** directive is used to show the contents of a specific section, whereas the **@section** directive, as its name suggests, defines a section of material.

Rendering Blade Templates

It may occasionally be necessary to convert a raw Blade template string into proper HTML. This may be done by utilizing the **Blade** facade's **render** method. The Blade template string and an optional array of data to feed the template are both accepted by the **render** method:

```
use Illuminate\Support\Facades\Blade;
```

```
return Blade::render('Welcome, {{ $name }}', ['name' => 'ABC']);
```

By writing the inline Blade templates to the **storage/framework/views** directory, Laravel renders them. You may provide the function the **deleteCachedView** argument if you want Laravel to delete these temporary files after rendering the Blade template:

```
return Blade::render(

    'Welcome, {{ $name }}',
    ['name' => 'ABC'],
```

```
    deleteCachedView: true


);
```

Rendering Blade Fragments

It may occasionally be necessary to just return a piece of a Blade template within your HTTP response when utilizing frontend frameworks like Turbo and htmx. You may achieve it by using blade **fragments**. Place a section of your Blade template inside the **@fragment** and **@endfragment** directives to get started:

```
@fragment('employee-list')

    <ul>
        @foreach ($employees as $employee)

            <li>{{ $employee->name }}</li>

        @endforeach
    </ul>

@endfragment
```

Then, you can use the **fragment** method to specify that just the given fragment should be included in the outgoing HTTP response when displaying the view that makes use of this template:

```
return view('homepage', ['employee' => $employees])->fragment
('employee-list');
```

By using the **fragmentIf** method, you may conditionally return a view fragment based on a specified condition. In such a case, the whole view will be returned:

```
return view('homepage', ['employees' => $employees])
    ->fragmentIf($request->hasHeader('HX-Request'), 'employee-list');
```

The two methods – **fragments** and **fragmentIf** – enable to return multiple view fragments in the response. For example:

```
view('homepage', ['employees' => $employee])
    ->fragments(['employee-list', 'task-list']);
```

```
view('homepage' ['employees' => $employees])
    ->fragmentsIf(

        $request->hasHeader('HX-Request'),
        ['employee-list', 'task-list']

    );
```

Conclusion

In this chapter, we explored the essential components of Laravel web development - Controllers and Blade templates. Controllers are important in the MVC architecture as they group the functionality of routes. We discussed how to create controllers using the Artisan command and how to manage actions for specific resources.

In the next chapter, we will delve into Eloquent and Query Builder in Laravel, which are essential for database operations. The upcoming chapter will also cover how to perform common Eloquent operations applied to the database using query builders.

Points to Remember

- Resource Controllers provide a convenient way to handle CRUD operations for multiple resources in an application, which is generated using the **make:controller** command. Routes are defined for resource controllers.

- Constructor injection and method injection, where dependencies are automatically resolved and injected into controller instances, providing clean and organized code.

- Redirects in Laravel are responses that send the user to a different URL. There are various ways to create redirects, including the Redirect Helper, named routes, and controller actions. Additionally, flashing session data is utilized for displaying success messages or preserving input data during redirects.

- Directives in Blade templates are instructions that execute specific logic or actions in the view. There are various types, including conditional directives, switch directives, and authentication directives like **@auth** and **@guest**, which help in managing user authentication in views.

- Loop directives in Blade, including **@for**, **@foreach**, **@forelse**, and **@while**, enable efficient handling of repetitive tasks and data display. The **@continue** and **@break** are used to skip iterations or exit loops when certain conditions are met.

- The **@once** directive allows a section of the template to be evaluated only once during rendering, which is useful for pushing specific content like JavaScript scripts to the header.

- Blade as a template engine in Laravel provides a clean and expressive way to create views with its mix of PHP and HTML. Components and layouts help in maintaining consistent designs across the application, making the code more modular and reusable.

- A comprehensive understanding of controllers and Blade templates in Laravel, equipping with essential tools fosr building robust and efficient web applications.

## CHAPTER 5

Working with Eloquent ORM and Query Builder

Introduction

This chapter covers Eloquent and Query Builder in Laravel, which are essential for database operations. It explains the importance of Eloquent and Query Builder in web development and how they are used in Laravel. The chapter also discusses how to perform common Eloquent operations applied to the database using query builders.

Structure

In this chapter, the following topics will be covered:

- Eloquent in Laravel
  - Conventions
- Eloquent Events
- Query Builder in Laravel
  - Selects
  - Joins
  - Advanced Where
  - Aggregates
  - Raw Expressions

        o Pessimistic Locking

        o Caching Queries

   • Eloquent Operations

        o Model Classes

        o Model Conventions

        o Retrieving Models

        o CRUD Operations on Models

        o Events

Eloquent in Laravel

Eloquent, an object-relational mapper (ORM) that makes it simple and accessible to interface with the application database, is a component of Laravel. Each database table in Eloquent has a matching **Model** that is used to communicate with the table. Eloquent models have the operations of inserting, editing, and removing records from the database table in addition to fetching them.

The `Illuminate\Database\Eloquent\Model` class is generally extended with models, which are normally located in the `app\Models` directory. To create a new model, use the `make:model` Artisan command:

```
php artisan make:model Car
```

When creating a new model and there is a requirement to generate a database migration, use the **`--migration`** or `-m` option.

When creating a model, you can also create different classes such as factories, seeders, policies, controllers, and form requests. Additionally, by combining these choices, it is possible to create numerous classes at once:

```
# Generate a model and a CarFactory class
php artisan make:model Car --factory
php artisan make:model Car -f
```

A factory is a way to define the structure and attributes of data that can be used for testing and database seeding.

```
# Generate a model and a CarSeeder class
php artisan make:model Car --seed
php artisan make:model Car -s


# Generate a model and a CarController class
php artisan make:model Car --controller
php artisan make:model Car -c


# Generate a model, CarController resource class, and form request
classes
php artisan make:model Car --controller --resource --requests
php artisan make:model Car -crR


# Generate a model and a CarPolicy class
php artisan make:model Car --policy


# Generate a model and a migration, factory, seeder, and controller
php artisan make:model Car -mfsc


# Shortcut to generate a model, migration, factory, seeder, policy,
controller, and form requests
php artisan make:model Car --all


# Generate a pivot model
php artisan make:model Member --pivot
php artisan make:model Member -p
```

Database Migrations

Database migrations play a crucial role in managing version control for databases, allowing your team to formulate and distribute the schema definition for the application's database. If you've ever encountered the challenge of instructing a team member to manually integrate a new column into their local database schema after pulling your changes from source control, you've likely grappled with the problem that database migrations aim to solve.

The Laravel Schema facade offers a versatile solution for creating and manipulating tables in a manner that is independent of the underlying database system. This facade is commonly employed in migrations to facilitate the creation and modification of database tables and columns across all of Laravel's supported database systems.

To create a database migration, use the `make:migration` Artisan command. The newly created migration will be saved in your `database/migrations` directory. Each migration filename has a date, which helps Laravel to identify the migrations' order:

```
php artisan make:migration create_cars_table
```

Laravel endeavors to predict the table name and determine whether a migration will generate a new table by analyzing the migration's name. If Laravel can deduce the table name from the migration name, it automatically populates the created migration file with the identified table. However, if the table name cannot be inferred, you have the option to explicitly specify the table within the migration file.

When employing the `make:migration` command, you have the flexibility to utilize the `--path` option to designate a particular path for the resultant migration. The specified path should be relative to your application's base path.

Primary Key

Eloquent will additionally presume that the associated database table for each model contains an `id` primary key field. If required, you may designate a different column as your model's main key by creating a protected `$primaryKey` property on your model:

```
<?php

namespace App\Models;
```

```
use Illuminate\Database\Eloquent\Model;


class Car extends Model
{
    /*
     * The primary key associated with the table.
     *
     * @var string
     */
    protected $primaryKey = 'car_id';
}
```

Each model must have at least one **ID** that may act as its primary key according to Eloquent. Eloquent models do not allow **composite** main keys. However, in addition to the main key that uniquely identifies the table, you are allowed to add other multi-column, unique indexes to your database tables.

Timestamps

By default, Eloquent anticipates the associated database table for your model to have the fields **created_at** and **updated_at**. When models are made or changed, Eloquent will automatically set the values for these columns. You should set the **$timestamps** property on your model to **false** if you do not want Eloquent to manage these columns automatically:

```php
<?php


namespace App\Models;


use Illuminate\Database\Eloquent\Model;


class Car extends Model
{
    /*
     * Indicates if the model should be timestamped.
```

```
    *
    * @var bool
    */


    public $timestamps = false;
}
```

You can work on the model within a closure provided by the **withoutTimestamps** function if you don't want the model's **updated_at** timestamp to be changed while you're working on it.

Eloquent Events

The different events in the lifecycle of an Eloquent can be used in any logical order and are as follows:

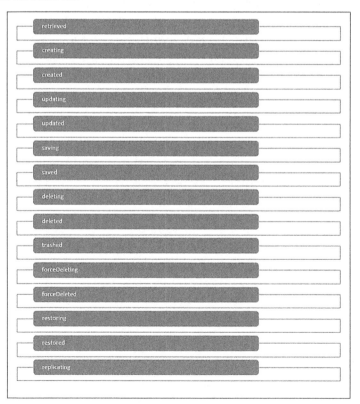

Figure 5.1: *Eloquent Events*

When a current model is obtained from the database, the retrieved event will be sent. The creating and created events will be dispatched when a new model is stored for the first time. When an existing model is changed and the save method is invoked, the updating/updated events will be dispatched. When a model is created or modified, even if its characteristics have not changed, the saving/saved events will be dispatched.

Events with names that end in **-ing** are sent out before any model changes are saved, whereas events with names that end in **-ed** are sent out once the changes to the model have been saved.

For instance, create a **$dispatchesEvents** property on your Eloquent model to begin receiving model events. This property associates your own event classes with various phases of the Eloquent model's lifecycle. Each model event class should anticipate receiving a constructor call from the impacted model's instance:

```php
<?php

namespace App\Models;

use App\Events\UserDeleted;
use App\Events\UserSaved;
use Illuminate\Foundation\Auth\User as Authenticatable;
use Illuminate\Notifications\Notifiable;

class User extends Authenticatable
{
    use Notifiable;

    /*
     * The event map for the model.
     *
     * @var array
     */
```

```
    protected $dispatchesEvents = [
        'saved' => UserSaved::class,
        'deleted' => UserDeleted::class,
    ];
}
```

(**Source**: Laravel.com/docs)

Query Builder in Laravel

Query Builder is one of the Laravel Framework's most crucial features. The database query builder provided by the Laravel framework provides a simple and intuitive interface for developing and using database queries. The majority of database activities in the application may be carried out using this method, and it works with all database systems supported by the Laravel Framework. To safeguard the application from any SQL injection threats, it is built on PDO parameter binding.

PDO parameter binding is used extensively throughout the Laravel query builder to defend your application from SQL injection threats. Strings passed as bindings do not need to be cleaned.

Selects

Selects are used to retrieve data in a Laravel application. In understanding Query Builder, we will look into the Employee Database scenario.

To fetch all rows:

```
$employees = DB::table('employees')->get();

foreach ($employees as $employee)
{
    var_dump($employee->name);
}
```

To fetch a single row:

```
$employee = DB::table('employees')->where('name', 'ABC')->first();

var_dump($employee->name);
```

To fetch a single column:

```
$employee = DB::table('employees')->where('name', 'ABC')
->pluck('name');
```

Select Clause:

```
$employees = DB::table('employees')->select('name', 'email')
->get();

$employees = DB::table('employees')->distinct()->get();

$employees = DB::table('employees')->select('name as
employeeName')->get();
```

OR Statements:

```
$employees = DB::table('employees')
                        ->where('employedDays', '>', 180)
                        ->orWhere('name', 'ABC')
                        ->get();
```

OrderBy, GroupBy, and having:

```
$employees = DB::table('employees')
                    ->orderBy('name', 'desc')
                    ->groupBy('count')
```

```
                        ->having('count', '>', 180)
                        ->get();
```

Joins

Based on a shared column between two or more columns, a JOIN clause is used to merge rows from those tables.

Syntax with an example:

```
DB::table('employees')
            ->join('contacts', 'employees.id', '=', 'contacts.
employee _id')
            ->join('orders', 'employees.id', '=', 'orders.
employee _id')
            ->select('employees.id', 'contacts.phone', 'orders.
price')
            ->get();
```

Left Join

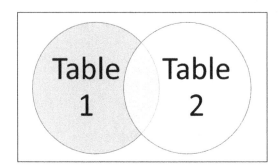

Figure 5.2: *Left Join*

To implement a join in code, refer to the following code example:

```
DB::table('employees')
        ->leftJoin('posts', 'employees.id', '=', 'posts. employee
_id')
        ->get();
```

Advanced Joins

Use the `where` and `orWhere` methods on a join if you want to employ a **where** style clause on your joins. These techniques test the column against a value rather than two columns:

```
DB::table('employees')
        ->join('contacts', function($join)
        {
            $join->on('employees.id', '=', 'contacts.employee_id')
                ->where('contacts.employee_id', '>', 10);
        })
        ->get();
```

Advanced Where

More complex `where` clauses, such as **where exists** or nested parameter groupings, could occasionally be required. These can also be handled by the Laravel query builder:

```
DB::table('employees')
            ->where('name', '=', 'ABC')
            ->orWhere(function($query)
            {
                $query->where('votes', '>', 100)
                    ->where('title', '<>', 'Admin');
            })
            ->get();
```

The aforementioned query will return the following SQL:

```
select * from employees where name = 'ABC' or (votes > 100 and title <>
'Admin')
```

Aggregates

A wide range of aggregate techniques, including **count**, `max`, `min`, **average**, and **total**, are now available in the query builder.

Count:

```
$employees = DB::table('employees')->count();
```

Max:

```
$cost = DB::table('orders')->max('cost');
```

Min:

```
$cost = DB::table('orders')->min('cost');
```

Average:

```
$cost = DB::table('orders')->avg('cost');
```

Sum:

```
$total = DB::table('employees')->sum('votes');
```

Raw Expressions

A query may occasionally need the usage of a raw expression. Take caution not to construct any SQL injection points because these expressions will be injected into the query as strings! You can use the **DB::raw** command to produce a raw expression:

```
$employees = DB::table('employees')
                ->select(DB::raw('count(*) as employee_count, sta-
tus'))
                ->where('status', '<>', 1)
                ->groupBy('status')
                ->get();
```

Pessimistic Locking

There are a few functions in the query builder that will assist you with **pessimistic locking** for your SELECT statements.

Use the `sharedLock` method on a query to execute the SELECT statement with a **shared lock**:

```
DB::table('employees')->where('votes', '>', 140)->
sharedLock()->get();
```

You can use the `lockForUpdate` method on a query to **lock for update** on a SELECT statement:

```
DB::table('employees')->where('votes', '>', 140)->
lockForUpdate()->get();
```

Caching Queries

Using the `remember or rememberForever` technique, you can conveniently cache a query's results:

```
$value = Cache::rememberForever('employees', function () {
    return DB::table('employees')->get();
});
```

This will retrieve it from the cache if it exists or store it forever if it does not exist.

Eloquent Operations

Eloquent, an object-relational mapper (ORM) that makes working with your database fun, is a component of Laravel. Each database table in Eloquent has a corresponding **Model** that is used to communicate with the table. Eloquent models allow you to insert, edit, and delete records from the database table in addition to fetching them.

Model Classes

Let's start by building an Eloquent model. The **Illuminate\Database\Eloquent\Model** class is generally extended with models, which are typically located in the **app\Models** directory. You could use the model Artisan command **make:model** to create a new model:

```
php artisan make:model Office
```

Use the **--migration** or **-m** option to generate a database model:

```
php artisan make:model Office --migration
```

When creating a model, you may also create different classes such as factories, seeders, policies, controllers, and form requests. Additionally, by combining these choices, it is possible to create numerous classes at once:

```
# Generate a model and a OfficeFactory class...
php artisan make:model Office --factory
php artisan make:model Office -f


# Generate a model and a OfficeSeeder class...
php artisan make:model Office --seed
php artisan make:model Office -s


# Generate a model and a OfficeController class...
php artisan make:model Office --controller
php artisan make:model Office -c


# Generate a model, OfficeController resource class, and form request
classes...
php artisan make:model Office --controller --resource --requests
php artisan make:model Office -crR
```

```
# Generate a model and a OfficePolicy class...
php artisan make:model Office --policy


# Generate a model and a migration, factory, seeder, and controller...
php artisan make:model Office -mfsc


# Shortcut to generate a model, migration, factory, seeder, policy,
controller, and form requests...
php artisan make:model Office --all


# Generate a pivot model...
php artisan make:model Member --pivot
php artisan make:model Member -p
```

Model Conventions

The **app/Models** directory will house any models created by the **make:model** command. Let's look at a fundamental model class and talk about some of Eloquent's fundamental conventions:

```php
<?php

namespace App\Models;

use Illuminate\Database\Eloquent\Model;

class Office extends Model
{
    // Code Logic
}
```

Table Name

You might have noted from the preceding example that we did not specify to Eloquent which database table corresponds to our **Office** model. Conventionally, unless another name is specifically supplied, the table name will be the class's **snake case**, plural name. Since an **OfficeCapacityController** model would store entries in a table called **office_capacity_controllers**, Eloquent will presume that the **Office** model stores records in the **office** table.

If the database table that corresponds to your model does not follow this norm, you can define a **table** attribute on the model to manually specify the table name:

```php
<?php

namespace App\Models;

use Illuminate\Database\Eloquent\Model;

class Office extends Model
{
    /**
     * The table associated with the model. And the logic.
     *
     * @var string
     *
     */
    protected $table = 'my_offices';
}
```

Primary Key

Eloquent will additionally presume that the associated database table for each model contains an **id** primary key column.

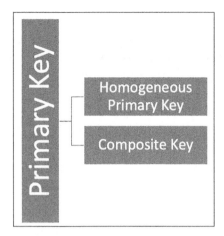

Figure 5.3: *Primary Key Types*

Homogeneous Primary Key

Eloquent will additionally presume that the associated database table for each model contains an **id** primary key column - **$primaryKey**:

```php
<?php

namespace App\Models;

use Illuminate\Database\Eloquent\Model;

class Office extends Model
{
    /**
     * The primary key associated with the table.
     *
     * @var string
     */
    protected $primaryKey = 'office_id';
}
```

Moreover, Eloquent will automatically convert the primary key to an integer because it expects that the primary key is an incrementing integer value. You must declare a public **$incrementing** property on your model with the value set to **false** if you want to utilize a non-incrementing or non-numeric primary key:

```php
<?php

class Office extends Model
{
    /**
     * Indicates if the model's ID is auto-incrementing.
     *
     * @var bool
     *
     */
    public $incrementing = false;
}
```

You should add a protected **$keyType** property to your model if the primary key is not an integer. The **String** should be the value for this property:

```php
<?php

class Office extends Model
{
    /**
     * The data type of the auto-incrementing ID.
     *
     * @var string
     *
     */
    protected $keyType = 'string';
}
```

Composite Primary Key

Each model must have at least one **ID** that can act as its primary key according to Eloquent. Eloquent models do not support **composite** main keys.

However, in addition to the main key that uniquely identifies the table, you are allowed to add other multi-column, unique indexes to your database tables.

UUID and ULID Keys

You may decide to utilize UUIDs as your Eloquent model's main keys rather than auto-incrementing integers. UUIDs are 36-character-long, globally unique alphanumeric identifiers.

Utilize the **Illuminate\Database\Eloquent\Concerns\HasUuids** trait on the model if you want a model to utilize a UUID key rather than an auto-incrementing integer key. Of course, you need to make sure that the model has a primary key column with a UUID equivalent:

```
use Illuminate\Database\Eloquent\Concerns\HasUuids;
use Illuminate\Database\Eloquent\Model;


class Chapter extends Model
{
    use HasUuids;


    // Code logic
}


$chapter = Chapter::create(['title' => 'Chapter 1']);


$chapter>id;
```

The **HasUuids** trait creates **ordered** UUIDs by default for your models. These UUIDs can be sorted lexicographically, making them more effective for index database storage:

By adding a **newUniqueId** function to a model, you can modify how a UUID is generated for that particular model. Additionally, you may define a **uniqueIds** function on the model to indicate which columns should get UUIDs:

```
use Ramsey\Uuid\Uuid;

/**
 * Generate a new UUID for the model.
 */

public function newUniqueId(): string
{
    return (string) Uuid::uuid4();
}

/**
 * Get the columns that should receive a unique identifier.
 *
 * @return array<int, string>
 *
 */

public function uniqueIds(): array
{
    return ['id', 'offer_code'];
}
```

You are free to use **ULIDs** instead of UUIDs if you choose. ULIDs are identical to UUIDs; however, they only have 26 characters. ULIDs can be lexicographically sorted for effective database indexing, just like ordered UUIDs.

Use the **Illuminate\Database\Eloquent\Concerns\HasUlids** trait on your model to make use of ULIDs. Additionally, make sure the model contains a main key column that is equivalent to ULID.

Database Connections

All Eloquent models will automatically use the default database connection set up for your application. You should define a **$connection** property on the model if you want to specify a different connection to be utilized when interacting with a specific model:

```php
<?php

namespace App\Models;

use Illuminate\Database\Eloquent\Model;

class Office extends Model
{
    /**
     * The database connection that should be used by the model.
     *
     * @var string
     *
     * Code Logic
     */
    protected $connection = 'sqlite';
}
```

Retrieving Models

You are prepared to begin data retrieval from your database once you have generated a model and the corresponding database table. Each Eloquent model may be viewed as a potent query builder that enables you to fluidly query the database table connected to the model. The model's **all** method will get every entry from the database table it's linked to:

```
use App\Models\Office;

foreach (Office::all() as $office) {

    echo $office->name;

}
```

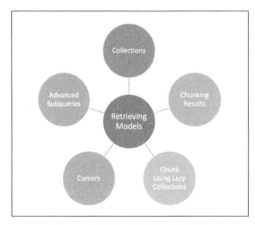

Figure 5.4: *Retrieving Models*

Collections

The fundamental **Illuminate\Support\Collection** class from Laravel, which offers a number of useful methods for interacting with data collections, is extended by the **Eloquent** Collection class. For instance, based on the outcomes of an invoked closure, the **reject** method may be used to delete models from a collection:

```
$offices = Office::where('location', 'NYC')->get();

$offices = $offices->reject(function (Office $office) {

    return $office->cancelled;
```

```
});
```

The Eloquent collection class has a few extra methods in addition to those offered by Laravel's standard collection class that are specifically designed for working with collections of Eloquent models.

You may loop over collections as if they were an array because Laravel's collections all adhere to PHP's iterable interfaces:

```
foreach ($offices as $office) {

    echo $office->id;

}
```

Chunking Results

If you try to use the **all** or **get** methods to load tens of thousands of Eloquent entries, your application can run out of memory. The **chunk** method can be used to process a lot of models more quickly than these other techniques.

A closure will receive a subset of Eloquent models that were retrieved by the **chunk** method and processed. When working with a large number of models, the **chunk** approach will result in much less memory use because just the most recent chunk of Eloquent models is obtained at a time:

```
use App\Models\Office;

use Illuminate\Database\Eloquent\Collection;

Office::chunk(200, function (Collection $offices) {

    foreach ($offices as $office) {

        // Code Logic
```

```
    }

});
```

The number of records you desire to receive each **chunk** is the first input supplied to the **chunk** method. For each chunk that is retrieved from the database, the closure supplied as the second parameter will be called. Each chunk of records supplied to the closure will be retrieved using a database query.

Use the **chunkById** method if you want to filter the outcomes of the **chunk** method based on a column that will also be updated when you iterate through the outcomes. In some situations, applying the **chunk** technique could produce erroneous or inconsistent outcomes. Internally, the **chunkById** method will always return models whose last model in the chunk's previous chunk has an **id** column larger than zero:

```
Office::where('closed', true)

    ->chunkById(200, function (Collection $offices) {

        $offices->each->update(['closed' => false]);

    }, $column = 'id');
```

Chunk Using Lazy Collections

In that it conducts the query in pieces behind the scenes, the **lazy** method functions similarly to the **chunk** method. However, the **lazy** method returns a flattened **LazyCollection** of Eloquent models, allowing you to interact with the results as a single stream rather than simply handing each chunk into a callback as is:

```
use App\Models\Office;

foreach (Office::lazy() as $office) {
```

```
// Code Logic


}
```

Use the **lazyById** method if you want to filter the outcomes of the **lazy** method based on a column that will also be updated as you iterate over the outcomes. Internally, the **lazyById** method will always return models whose **id** columns are bigger than the ones of the last model in the **chunk** before:

```
Office::where('closed', true)


    ->lazyById(200, $column = 'id')


    ->each->update(['closed' => false]);
```

The **lazyByIdDesc** method allows you to filter the results based on the **id's** descending order.

Cursors

The **cursor** method can be used to drastically reduce your application's memory consumption when iterating through tens of thousands of Eloquent model records, similar to the **lazy** method.

Individual Eloquent models won't be hydrated until they are iterated through; the **cursor** technique will only run one database query. As a result, while iterating over the cursor, only one Eloquent model is retained in memory at any given time.

Internally, the **cursor** method implements the following features using PHP generators:

```
use App\Models\Office;


foreach (Office::where('location, 'NYC')->cursor() as $office) {


    //Code Logic
```

```
}
```

An Illuminate\Support\LazyCollection instance is returned by the **cursor**. While only loading one model into memory at a time, lazy collections let you utilize many of the collection methods offered by standard Laravel collections:

```
use App\Models\User;

$users = User::cursor()->filter(function (User $user) {

    return $user->age > 18;

});

foreach ($users as $user) {

    echo $user->name;

}
```

Because it only keeps one Eloquent model in memory at a time, the **cursor** technique consumes far less memory than a standard query, but it will ultimately run out of space. This is because PHP's PDO driver stores all raw query results in its internal buffer. Consider switching to the lazy technique if you're working with a lot of Eloquent records.

Advanced Subqueries

We can select all of the **locations** and the name of the office at each location using a single query by leveraging the subquery functionality offered by the query builder's **select** and **addSelect** methods:

```
use App\Models\Location;
use App\Models\Office;
```

```
return Location::addSelect(['last_office' => Office::select('name')

    ->whereColumn('Location_id', 'locations.id')

    ->orderByDesc('Location_id')

    ->limit(1)

])->get();
```

Additionally, subqueries are supported by the **orderBy** function of the query builder. Using our office as an example, we can utilize this functionality to arrange all locations by the time the most recent office was added/constructed there.

CRUD Operations on Models

While using Eloquent, it is important not only to fetch models from the database but also to add new records. Fortunately, Eloquent makes it easy. You just need to create a new model instance, specify its characteristics, and then insert a new record into the database using the model instance's **save** method:

```php
<?php

namespace App\Http\Controllers;

use App\Http\Controllers\Controller;
use App\Models\Office;
use Illuminate\Http\RedirectResponse;
use Illuminate\Http\Request;

class OfficeController extends Controller
{
    /**
     * Store a new Office in the database.
     */
```

```
public function store(Request $request): RedirectResponse
{
    // Validate the request...

    $office = new Office;

    $office->name = $request->name;

    $office->save();

    return redirect('/offices');
}
}
```

Models that already exist in the database can be updated using the **save** technique. A model should be retrieved in order to be updated, then any desired characteristics should be set. The **save** method for the model should then be called. Again, there is no need to explicitly specify the value of the **updated_at** timestamp because it will be updated automatically:

```
use App\Models\Office;

$office  = Office::find(1);

$office ->name = 'SFO';

$office ->save();
```

You may use the model instance's **delete** function to remove a model:

```
use App\Models\Office;

$office = Office::find(1);
```

```
$office->delete();
```

Events

Eloquent models send out various events, allowing you to hook into the following lifecycle events:

1. retrieved
2. creating
3. created
4. updating
5. updated
6. saving
7. saved
8. deleting
9. deleted
10. trashed
11. forceDeleting
12. forceDeleted
13. restoring
14. restored
15. replicating

Use observers to categorize all of your listeners into a single class if you are listening for a lot of events on a certain model. The Eloquent events you want to listen for are reflected in the method names of the observer classes. The impacted model is the sole argument for each of these methods. The simplest method to build a new observer class is to use the **make:observer** Artisan command:

```
php artisan make:observer UserObserver --model=Employee
```

The new observer will be added to the **app/Observers** directory by this command. Artisan will create this directory for you if it does not already exist. Your impartial observer will look as follows:

```php
<?php

namespace App\Observers;

use App\Models\Employee;

class EmployeeObserver
{
    /**
     * Handle the Employee "created" event.
     */
    public function created(Employee $employee): void
    {
        // Code Logic
    }

    /**
     * Handle the Employee "updated" event.
     */
    public function updated(User $employee): void
    {
        // Code Logic
    }

    /**
     * Handle the User "deleted" event.
     */
    public function deleted(User $user): void
    {
```

```
    // ...
}


/**
 * Handle the Employee "restored" event.
 */
public function restored(User $employee): void
{
    // Code Logic
}


/**
 * Handle the Employee "forceDeleted" event.
 */
public function forceDeleted(User $employee): void
{
    // Code Logic
}
}
```

At times, you might need to **mute** a model's whole firing of events. This can be achieved by utilizing the **withoutEvents** technique. The only input for the **withoutEvents** function is a closure. The **withoutEvents** function will return any result returned by the closure, and any code performed within this closure won't dispatch model events.

Conclusion

In this chapter, *Working with Eloquent ORM and Query Builder*, the focus was on exploring the fundamental concepts of Eloquent ORM and Query Builder in the context of Laravel, a popular PHP framework for web development. The chapter began by introducing the importance of Eloquent and Query Builder in database operations within web development projects.

The chapter's goal was to provide readers with a thorough grasp of Laravel's Eloquent ORM and Query Builder while highlighting their significance and illuminating how to use them through real-world scenarios. It discussed key ideas and methods that programmers may use to create effective and dependable database-driven Laravel applications.

In the next chapter, we will look at the security aspects of the Laravel application, including how to incorporate authentication and authorization in Laravel.

Points to Remember

- Eloquent ORM simplifies database operations in Laravel by providing an object-oriented interface to interact with database tables.
- Each database table in Eloquent corresponds to a **Model** class that communicates with the table.
- Models can perform insert, update, delete, and fetch operations on records.
- Use the `make:model` Artisan command to create a new model.
- Models follow naming conventions for table names and primary keys. You can customize these using properties like `$table` and `$primaryKey`.
- You can retrieve data using methods like `get()`, `first()`, and `pluck()`.
- Joins merge rows from different tables based on shared columns.
- Aggregates like count, max, min, average, and sum can be used to perform calculations on columns.
- Collections are extended arrays that allow various manipulation methods.
- Chunking results and using cursors help manage memory consumption when dealing with large datasets.
- CRUD operations involve creating, updating, and deleting records using the model's instance.
- Eloquent models emit events during their lifecycle, such as creating, updating, and deleting.
- Event classes can be created to handle specific model events.
- The `$dispatchesEvents` property associates event classes with model events.
- Eloquent events provide hooks for executing custom logic during various phases of a model's lifecycle.

## CHAPTER 6

Implementing Authentication and Authorization in Laravel

Introduction

This chapter will focus on how to handle user authentication, set up registration and login pages, and create a password reset flow. You will also learn how to implement user authorization, define roles and permissions, and create policies and gates to manage access to resources. This chapter will also cover best practices for storing passwords and securing user data.

Structure

In this chapter, the following topics will be covered:

- Laravel's built-in authentication system
  - Laravel API authentication services
  - Passport
  - Sanctum

- Customizing authentication and registration logic
  - HTTP authentication
  - Stateless HTTP authentication
  - Custom user providers
- Implementing authorization policies and gates
  - Invalidating user sessions
  - Password management
  - Authentication custom guards
  - Authenticatable contract
  - Invalidate sessions across multiple devices
  - User session knowledge
  - Additional authentication methods
- Securing routes and actions with middleware
  - Middleware
  - Assigning middleware to routes
  - Middleware groups
  - Sorting middleware
  - Middleware parameters
  - Terminable middleware

Laravel's built-in Authentication System

Many online apps include a method for users to **login** and authenticate with the program. This feature's implementation in web applications can be a challenging and perhaps dangerous task. Laravel makes an effort to provide you with the resources you need to create authentication quickly, safely, and simply.

The **guards** and **providers** at the center of Laravel's authentication infrastructure make up the system. Guards specify the user authentication process for each request. For instance, Laravel has a `session` guard that uses cookies and session storage to retain state.

Users are fetched from your persistent storage via providers. Laravel includes Eloquent and the database query builder functionality for fetching users. You may, however, establish more providers as needed for your application.

The authentication configuration file for your application is located at **config/auth.php**. This file includes a number of well-documented options for modifying the behavior of Laravel's authentication services.

Laravel API Authentication Services

Passport and Sanctum are two optional packages provided by Laravel to help you manage API tokens and authenticate requests performed with API tokens. Please keep in mind that these libraries and the built-in cookie-based authentication libraries in Laravel are not mutually exclusive. These libraries are primarily concerned with API token authentication, whereas the built-in authentication services are concerned with cookie-based browser authentication. Many applications will make use of both Laravel's built-in cookie-based authentication and one of Laravel's API authentication packages.

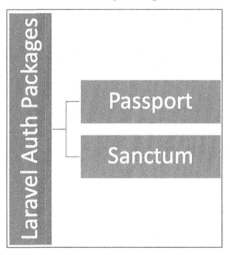

Figure 6.1: *Laravel Auth Packages*

In addition to Passport and Sanctum, Laravel also has Laravel Fortify that can be used for authentication. Laravel Fortify is a Laravel authentication backend implementation that is not dependent on the front end. Fortify registers the routes and controllers required to implement all of Laravel's authentication capabilities, including login, registration, password reset, and email verification.

Passport

Passport is an OAuth2 authentication provider that provides a number of OAuth2 "grant types" that allow you to issue different sorts of tokens. In general, this is a comprehensive and complicated API authentication package.

Most apps, however, do not require the extensive functionalities provided by the OAuth2 spec, which can be perplexing for both users and developers. Furthermore, developers have previously been perplexed as to how to authenticate SPA apps or mobile applications utilizing OAuth2 authentication providers, such as Passport.

Sanctum

Laravel Sanctum is an authentication package that solves a number of problems faced in developing Laravel applications. The package is a more streamlined package that is capable of handling first-party web requests as well as API calls made through tokens. This also helps remove the complexity of OAuth2.

In addition to being an API, it offers a first-party web UI, which means that SPA (single-page applications) exists independent of the backend Laravel application and independent of the mobile client.

Laravel Sanctum is a hybrid web/API authentication module that can handle the complete authentication process for your application. This is feasible because when Sanctum-based apps get a request, Sanctum first determines if the request has a session cookie referencing an authenticated session.

Sanctum achieves this by utilizing Laravel's built-in authentication services, as previously explained. Sanctum will check the request for an API token if it is not authenticated through a session cookie. If an API token is present, Sanctum will use that token to authenticate the request.

Customizing Authentication and Registration logic

To achieve custom authentication logic for the Laravel application, it is critical to incorporate HTTP authentication.

HTTP Authentication

HTTP Authentication allows you to quickly authenticate users of your application without having to build up a separate "login" page. Attach the `auth.basic` middleware to a route to get started. You do not need to define the `auth.basic` middleware because it is available with the Laravel framework.

```
Route::get('/profile', function () {

    // Only authenticated users may access this route

})->middleware('auth.basic');
```

When you access the route in your browser once the middleware has been attached, you will be requested for credentials. The **auth.basic** middleware will presume that the **email** field in your **users** database table is the user's "username" by default.

HTTP Basic authentication may fail if you use PHP FastCGI and Apache to serve your Laravel application. To resolve these issues, add the following lines to your application's **.htaccess** file:

```
RewriteCond %{HTTP:Authorization} ^(.+)$
RewriteRule .* - [E=HTTP_AUTHORIZATION:%{HTTP:Authorization}]
```

Stateless HTTP Authentication

You may also use HTTP Basic Authentication without setting a session identification cookie. This is especially useful if you use HTTP Authentication to authenticate calls to your application's API. To do so, create a middleware that calls the **onceBasic** function. If the **onceBasic** function returns no answer, the request may be sent further through the application:

```php
<?php

namespace App\Http\Middleware;

use Closure;
use Illuminate\Http\Request;
use Illuminate\Support\Facades\Auth;
use Symfony\Component\HttpFoundation\Response;
```

```php
class AuthenticateBasicAuth
{
    /**
     * Handle an incoming request.
     *
     * @param  \Closure(\Illuminate\Http\Request): (\Symfony\Component\
HttpFoundation\Response)  $next
     */

    public function handle(Request $request, Closure $next): Response
    {
        return Auth::onceBasic() ?: $next($request);
    }

}
```

Additionally, attach a middleware to a route:

```php
Route::get('/api/user', function () {

    // Only authenticated users may access this route

})->middleware(AuthenticateBasicAuth::class);
```

Custom User Providers

If you are not storing your users in a standard relational database, you will need to extend Laravel with your own authentication user provider. To define a custom user provider, we will utilize the **provider** method on the **Auth** façade. The user provider resolver should return an **Illuminate\Contracts\Auth\UserProvider** implementation:

```php
<?php
```

```
namespace App\Providers;

use App\Extensions\TestEmployeeProvider;
use Illuminate\Contracts\Foundation\Application;
use Illuminate\Foundation\Support\Providers\AuthServiceProvider as
ServiceProvider;
use Illuminate\Support\Facades\Auth;

class AuthServiceProvider extends ServiceProvider
{
    /**
     * Register any application authentication / authorization services.
     */
    public function boot(): void
    {
        Auth::provider('test', function (Application $app, array $config)
{

            // Return an instance of Illuminate\Contracts\Auth\User
Provider

            return new TestEmployeeProvider($app->make('test.
connection'));

        });
    }
}
```

After you've registered the provider using the provider method, you may change your auth.php configuration file to utilize the new user provider. First, identify a provider that will make use of your new driver:

```
'providers' => [
```

```php
        'employees' => [

                'driver' => 'test',

        ],

],
```

Finally, you may use the following provider in your **guards** configuration:

```php
'guards' => [

        'web' => [

                'driver' => 'session',
                'provider' => 'employees',

        ],

],
```

User Provider Contract

Implementations of `Illuminate\Contracts\Auth\UserProvider` are in charge of retrieving an `Illuminate\Contracts\Auth\Authenticatable` implementation from a persistent storage system, such as MySQL, MongoDB, and so on. These two interfaces enable the Laravel authentication procedures to perform independently of how the user data is stored or what type of class is used to represent the authorized user:

Let us examine the `Illuminate\Contracts\Auth\UserProvider` contract:

```php
<?php

namespace Illuminate\Contracts\Auth;
```

```
interface UserProvider
{

    public function retrieveById($identifier);
    public function retrieveByToken($identifier, $token);
    public function updateRememberToken(Authenticatable $user, $token);
    public function retrieveByCredentials(array $credentials);
    public function validateCredentials(Authenticatable $user, array
$credentials);


}
```

The **retrieveById** method normally gets a key describing the user from a MySQL database, such as an auto-incrementing ID. The method should retrieve and return the **Authenticatable** implementation that matches the ID.

The **retrieveByToken** method returns a user based on their unique **$identifier** and "remember me" **$token**, which is normally kept in a database column called **remember_token**. This method, like the last one, should return the **Authenticatable** implementation with a matched token value.

The **updateRememberToken** function replaces the **remember_token** of the **$user** object with the updated **$token**. After a successful "remember me" authentication attempt or when the user logs out, a new token is assigned to the user.

When attempting to authenticate with an application, the **retrieveByCredentials** function accepts the array of credentials supplied to the **Auth::attempt** method. The procedure should then "query" the underlying persistent storage for the user whose credentials match those provided. This function will often execute a query with a "where" condition that looks for a user record with a "username" that matches the value of **$credentials['username']**. The method should return an **Authenticatable** implementation. This method should not attempt to validate or authenticate passwords.

To authenticate the user, the **validateCredentials** function should match the provided **$user** to the **$credentials**. For example, to compare the value of **$user->getAuthPassword()** to the value of **$credentials['password']**, this function will often utilize the **Hash::check** method. This method should return **true** or **false** depending on whether it is valid.

Authenticatable Contract

Now that we've gone over each function on the **UserProvider**, let's look at the **Authenticatable** contract.

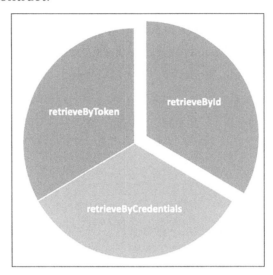

Figure 6.2: *Authenticable Contract Return Values*

Remember that user providers should return these interface implementations from the **retrieveById**, **retrieveByToken**, and **retrieveByCredentials** methods.

```php
<?php

namespace Illuminate\Contracts\Auth;

interface Authenticatable

{

    public function getAuthIdentifierName();
    public function getAuthIdentifier();
    public function getAuthPassword();
    public function getRememberToken();
    public function setRememberToken($value);
    public function getRememberTokenName();
```

```
}
```

This interface is straightforward. The **getAuthIdentifierName** function should return the name of the user's **primary key** field, and the **getAuthIdentifier** method should return the user's **primary key.** When utilizing a MySQL backend, this is most likely the user record's auto-incrementing primary key. The **getAuthPassword** function should return the hashed password of the user.

This interface enables the authentication system to interact with any **user** class, independent of the ORM or storage abstraction layer used. Laravel provides an **App\Models\User** class in the **app/Models** directory by default, which implements this interface.

Implementing Authorization Policies and Gates

While incorporating security with authentication and authorization, a key aspect is to keep track of the users currently allowed into the system. The users who are authenticated and authorized should also be kept in check and have a policy defined to auto-logout and keep track of the session data.

You may use the Auth facade's logout function to manually log users out of your application. This removes the authentication information from the user's session, preventing future requests from being authenticated.

It is suggested that, in addition to invoking the logout function, you invalidate the user's session and renew their CSRF token. After logging the user out, you should normally redirect the user to the application's root:

```
use Illuminate\Http\Request;
use Illuminate\Http\RedirectResponse;
use Illuminate\Support\Facades\Auth;

/**
 * Log the user out of the application.
 */
```

```
public function logout(Request $request): RedirectResponse
{
    Auth::logout();

    $request->session()->invalidate();

    $request->session()->regenerateToken();

    return redirect('/home');
}
```

Invalidating User Sessions

Laravel also has a technique for invalidating and **logging** out a user's sessions that are active on other devices without invalidating their current session. When a user changes or updates their password, you may use this functionality to invalidate sessions on other devices while keeping the current device authorized.

Before you begin, ensure that the **Illuminate\Session\Middleware\ AuthenticateSession** middleware is present on the routes that should receive session authentication. This middleware should typically be placed on a route group definition so that it may be applied to the bulk of the application's routes. The **AuthenticateSession** middleware is associated with a route by default through the **auth.session** route middleware alias set in your application's HTTP kernel:

```
Route::middleware(['auth', 'auth.session'])->group(function () {

    Route::get('/', function () {

        // Code Logic

    });

});
```

Then, you may utilize the Auth facade's **logoutOtherDevices** function. This technique needs the user to validate their current password, which should be accepted by your application via an input form:

```
use Illuminate\Support\Facades\Auth;


Auth::logoutOtherDevices($currentPassword);
```

When the **logoutOtherDevices** method is called, all the user's prior sessions are invalidated, which means they are **logged out** of any guards they were previously authenticated by.

Password Management

You may have actions in your application that need the user to confirm their password before the action is done or before the user is routed to a sensitive region of the application. Laravel contains built-in middleware to make this procedure as simple as possible.

You will need to design two routes to implement this feature:

- Display a view requesting the user to confirm their password
- Ensure that the password is genuine and redirect the user to their desired destination

Configuration

After verifying their password, a user will not be prompted to do so again for three hours. You may, however, change the value of the **password_timeout** setting variable within your application's **config/auth.php** configuration file to customize the amount of time before the user is requested for their password.

Routing

First, we'll construct a route that will display a view asking the user to confirm their password:

```
Route::get('/confirmPassword', function () {
```

```
    return view('auth.confirm-password');


})->middleware('auth')->name('password.confirm');
```

As you may anticipate, the view provided by this route should have a form with a password field. In addition, feel free to put text within the view that informs the user that they are entering a secured part of the program and must confirm their password.

Following that, we'll construct a route to handle the form request from the "confirm password" page. This route will be in charge of confirming the user's password and forwarding them to their desired destination:

```
use Illuminate\Http\Request;

use Illuminate\Support\Facades\Hash;

use Illuminate\Support\Facades\Redirect;


Route::post('/confirmPassword', function (Request $request) {


    if (! Hash::check($request->password, $request->user()->password)) {


        return back()->withErrors([
            'password' => ['Incorrect Password']
        ]);
    }


    $request->session()->passwordConfirmed();


    return redirect()->intended();


})->middleware(['auth', 'throttle:6,1']);
```

Let's take a closer look at this path before going on. First, the request's **password** field is checked to see if it matches the password of the authorized user. If the password is correct, we must notify Laravel's session that the user has validated their password. The **passwordConfirmed** method adds a timestamp to the user's session, which Laravel may use to detect when the user last verified their password. Finally, we may guide the user to their desired location.

Authentication Custom Guards

Using the **extend** method on the Auth facade, you may create your own authentication guards. You should make a call to a service provider's **extend** method. Because Laravel already has an **AuthServiceProvider**, we can paste the following code into it:

```php
<?php

namespace App\Providers;

use App\Services\Auth\JwtGuard;
use Illuminate\Contracts\Foundation\Application;
use Illuminate\Foundation\Support\Providers\AuthServiceProvider as
ServiceProvider;
use Illuminate\Support\Facades\Auth;

class AuthServiceProvider extends ServiceProvider
{
    /**
     * Register any application authentication / authorization services.
     */

    public function boot(): void
    {
        Auth::extend('jwt', function (Application $app, string $name,
array $config) {

            // Return an instance of Illuminate\Contracts\Auth\Guard

            return new JwtGuard(Auth::createUserProvider($config
['provider']));
```

```
        });
    }
}
```

As seen in the preceding example, the callback supplied to the **extend** method should return an **Illuminate\Contracts\Auth\Guard** implementation. This interface provides a few methods that must be implemented to define a custom guard. Once you've defined your own guard, you can use it in the **guards** configuration of your **auth.php** configuration file:

```
'guards' => [
    'api' => [

        'driver' => 'jwt',
        'provider' => 'users',

    ],
],
```

Closure Request Guards

Using the **Auth::viaRequest** function is the simplest approach to construct a bespoke HTTP request-based authentication system. Using a single closure, you can easily create your authentication procedure.

To begin, invoke the **Auth::viaRequest** function from your **AuthServiceProvider**'s startup method. The first argument to the **viaRequest** method is the name of an authentication driver. Any string that describes your custom guard can be used as this name. The method's second parameter should be a closure that receives the incoming HTTP request and returns a user instance or **null** if authentication fails:

```
use App\Models\User;
use Illuminate\Http\Request;
use Illuminate\Support\Facades\Auth;

/**
```

```
 * Register any application authentication / authorization service
 */
public function boot(): void
{
    Auth::viaRequest('customToken', function (Request $request) {

        return Employee::where('token', (string) $request->
token)->first();

    });
}
```

Once your custom authentication driver has been developed, you can add it as a driver to your auth.php configuration file's guards configuration:

```
'guards' => [

    'api' => [

        'driver' => 'customToken',

    ],

],
```

Finally, when adding the authentication middleware to a route, you may refer to the guard:

```
Route::middleware('auth:api')->group(function () {

    // Code Logic

}
```

Invalidate Sessions across Multiple Devices

Laravel also has a technique for invalidating and "logging out" a user's sessions that are active on other devices without invalidating their current session. When a user changes or updates their password, you may use this functionality to invalidate sessions on other devices while keeping the current device authorized.

Before you begin, ensure that the **Illuminate\Session\Middleware\ AuthenticateSession** middleware is present on the routes that should receive session authentication. This middleware should typically be placed on a route group definition so that it may be applied to the bulk of your application's routes. The **AuthenticateSession** middleware is associated with a route by default through the **auth.session** route middleware alias set in your application's HTTP kernel:

```
Route::middleware(['auth', 'auth.session'])->group(function () {


    Route::get('/', function () {

        // Code Logic

    });


});
```

Then, you may utilize the **Auth** facade's **logoutOtherDevices** function. This technique needs the user to validate their current password, which should be accepted by your application via an input form:

```
use Illuminate\Support\Facades\Auth;


Auth::logoutOtherDevices($currentPassword);
```

When the **logoutOtherDevices** method is called, all the user's prior sessions are invalidated, which means they are "logged out" of any guards they were previously authenticated by.

User Session Knowledge

On their login form, many web apps have a `remember me` checkbox. You may include `remember me` functionality in your application by passing a boolean value as the second parameter to the try method.

When this value is set to **true**, Laravel will keep the user authorized indefinitely or until they log out manually. The string `remember_token` column in your **users** table must be present since it will be used to hold the "remember me" token. This field is already included in the user table migration bundled with new Laravel applications:

```
use Illuminate\Support\Facades\Auth;


if (Auth::attempt(['email' => $email, 'password' => $password],
$remember)) {


    // The user is saved


}
```

If your application supports remember me, you may use the `viaRemember` method to see if the currently authorized user was authenticated using the "remember me" cookie:

```
use Illuminate\Support\Facades\Auth;


if (Auth::viaRemember()) {


    // Code Logic


}
```

Additional Authentication Methods

In order to authenticate a user, in addition to the ways mentioned, there are a number of additional methods are available while developing the Laravel Application.

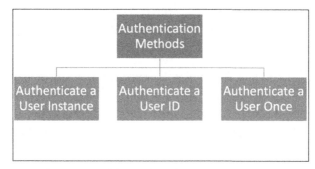

Figure 6.3: *Additional Authentication Methods*

Authenticate a User Instance

If you need to make an existing user instance, the currently authenticated user, you can utilize the Auth facade's login function. The provided user instance must be an **Illuminate\Contracts\Auth\Authenticatable** implementation. This interface is already implemented in the Laravel **App\Models\User** model. This authentication technique is handy when you already have a valid user instance, such as when a user registers with your application:

```
use Illuminate\Support\Facades\Auth;


Auth::login($user);
```

As the second argument to the login function, you can send a boolean value. This value determines whether the "remember me" capability for the authorized session is desired. Remember that the session will be authenticated continuously or until the user logs out of the application manually:

```
Auth::login($user, $remember = true);
```

If needed, you may specify an authentication guard before calling the login method:

```
Auth::guard('admin')->login($user);
```

Authenticate a User By ID

You may use the **loginUsingId** function to authenticate a user by utilizing the main key of their database record. This approach requires the main key of the user to be authenticated:

```
Auth::loginUsingId(5);
```

As the second argument to the **loginUsingId** function, you can send a boolean value. This value determines whether the "remember me" capability for the authorized session is desired. Remember that the session will be authenticated continuously or until the user logs out of the application manually:

```
Auth::loginUsingId(5, $remember = true);
```

Authenticate a User Once

To authenticate a user with the application for a single request, use the **once** method. When calling this method, no sessions or cookies will be used:

```
if (Auth::once($credentials)) {

    // Code Logic

}
```

Securing Routes and Actions with Middleware

Even though the check function may be used to ascertain whether a user is authenticated, you will usually employ a middleware to confirm that the user is authorized before granting access to specific routes or controllers.

It is possible to restrict access to a certain route to authorized users by using route middleware. A middleware for authentication that comes with Laravel makes use of the class **Illuminate\Auth\Middleware\Authenticate**. You just need to attach the middleware to a route specification because it is already registered in the HTTP kernel of your application:

```
Route::get('/offices', function () {

    // Only authenticated users logic

})->middleware('auth');
```

Middleware

Middleware offers an easy way to analyze and filter HTTP requests coming into your application. Laravel, for instance, comes with middleware that confirms the user of your application has been authenticated. The middleware will lead the user to your application's login screen if they have not been authorized. However, the middleware will permit the request to advance farther within the application if the user is authorized.

Other than authentication, other middleware may be created to carry out a range of activities. For instance, a logging middleware may log each request that comes through your application. The Laravel framework comes with a variety of middleware, such as middleware for CSRF protection and authentication. The **app/Http/Middleware** directory contains all of these middleware.

Use the **make:middleware** command to create a new middleware. crafter command

```
php artisan make:middleware EnsureTokenIsValid
```

A new instance of the **EnsureTokenIsValid** class will be created in the **app/Http/Middleware** directory by this operation. In this middleware, we only permit access to the route if the **token** input provided satisfies a predetermined value. If not, we will send users back to the **home** URL.

```
<?php
```

```php
namespace App\Http\Middleware;

use Closure;
use Illuminate\Http\Request;
use Symfony\Component\HttpFoundation\Response;

class EnsureTokenIsValid
{
    /**
     * Handle an incoming request.
     *
     * @param  \Closure(\Illuminate\Http\Request): (\Symfony\Component\
HttpFoundation\Response)  $next
     */
    public function handle(Request $request, Closure $next): Response
    {
        if ($request->input('token') !== 'secret-token') {

            return redirect('home');

        }

        return $next($request);
    }
}
```

As you can see, the middleware will send the client an HTTP redirect if the provided token does not match our secret **token**; otherwise, the request will be sent to the application. Calling the **$next** callback with the **$request** will transfer the request further into the application, letting the middleware "pass".

The easiest way to think of middleware is as a set of **layers** that HTTP requests must transit through before they can access your application. Each tier has the option to review the request or even reject it completely.

Before or after forwarding the request further into the application, a middleware might do our tasks. For instance, the middleware shown here would carry out a job before the application handles the request:

```php
<?php

namespace App\Http\Middleware;

use Closure;
use Illuminate\Http\Request;
use Symfony\Component\HttpFoundation\Response;

class BeforeMiddleware
{
    public function handle(Request $request, Closure $next): Response
    {
        // Perform action

        return $next($request);
    }
}
```
Source: *https://laravel.com/docs/*

However, this middleware would carry out its function after the application has dealt with the request:

```php
<?php

namespace App\Http\Middleware;

use Closure;
use Illuminate\Http\Request;
use Symfony\Component\HttpFoundation\Response;
```

```
class AfterMiddleware
{
    public function handle(Request $request, Closure $next): Response
    {
        $response = $next($request);

        // Perform action

        return $response;
    }
}
```
Source: https://laravel.com/docs/

Assigning Middleware To Routes

You may use the **middleware** method while specifying the route if you want to
apply middleware to particular routes:

```
use App\Http\Middleware\Authenticate;

Route::get('/EmployeeProfile', function () {

    // Code Logic

})->middleware(Authenticate::class);
```

By giving an array of middleware names to the **middleware** method, you may add
more than one middleware to the route:

```
Route::get('/', function () {

    // Code Logic

})->middleware([First::class, Second::class]);
```

You may give middleware aliases in your application's **app/Http/Kernel.php** file for convenience. The middleware that comes with Laravel is listed in the class's **$middlewareAliases** field by default. You are free to add your own middleware and give it whatever alias you like to this list:

```
// Within App\Http\Kernel class...

protected $middlewareAliases = [
    'auth' => \App\Http\Middleware\Authenticate::class,

    'auth.basic' => \Illuminate\Auth\Middleware\AuthenticateWithBasic
Auth::class,

    'bindings' => \Illuminate\Routing\Middleware\Substitute
Bindings::class,

    'cache.headers' => \Illuminate\Http\Middleware\SetCache
Headers::class,

    'allowed' => \Illuminate\Auth\Middleware\Authorize::class,

    'guest' => \App\Http\Middleware\RedirectIfAuthenticated::class,

    'signed' => \Illuminate\Routing\Middleware\ValidateSignature::class,

    'throttle' => \Illuminate\Routing\Middleware\Throttle
Requests::class,

    'verified' => \Illuminate\Auth\Middleware\EnsureEmailIs
Verified::class,

];
```

When adding middleware to routes, you can utilize the middleware alias that has been specified in the HTTP kernel.

```
Route::get('/EmployeeProfile', function () {

    // Code Logic

})->middleware('auth');
```

Middleware Groups

To make it simpler to attach middleware to routes, you might occasionally wish to aggregate several middleware under a single key. The **$middlewareGroups** property of your HTTP kernel may be used to do this.

The web and API middleware groups that Laravel pre-defines contain common middleware that you might wish to use on your **web** and **API** routes. Keep in mind that the following middleware groups are automatically applied to the routes in your relevant **web** and **api** route files by your application's **App\Providers\ RouteServiceProvider** service provider:

```
/**
 * The application's route middleware groups.
 *
 * @var array
 */
protected $middlewareGroups = [

    'web' => [

        \App\Http\Middleware\EncryptCookies::class,

        \Illuminate\Cookie\Middleware\AddQueuedCookiesToResponse::class,

        \Illuminate\Session\Middleware\StartSession::class,
```

```
    \Illuminate\View\Middleware\ShareErrorsFromSession::class,

    \App\Http\Middleware\VerifyCsrfToken::class,

    \Illuminate\Routing\Middleware\SubstituteBindings::class,
],

'api' => [

    \Illuminate\Routing\Middleware\ThrottleRequests::class.':api',

    \Illuminate\Routing\Middleware\SubstituteBindings::class,

],
];
```

In order to assign the middleware groups, the syntax remains similar to that of linking middleware to the routes and controllers. This helps in enabling the logic in our Laravel application code and also attaching the middleware to a route.

```
Route::get('/', function () {

    // Code Logic

})->middleware('web');

Route::middleware(['web'])->group(function () {

    // Code Logic

});
```

The **App\Providers\RouteServiceProvider** automatically applies the **web** and **api** middleware groups to the respective **routes/web.php** and **routes/api.php** files in your application right out of the box.

Sorting Middleware

Rarely, you could require your middleware to run in a precise sequence, but you wouldn't have control over the order in which they appear when they are assigned to the route. In this situation, the **$middlewarePriority** property of your **app/Http/Kernel.php** file may be used to indicate your middleware priority.

Your HTTP kernel may not, by default, have this attribute. You can duplicate its default definition if it doesn't already exist:

```
/**
 * The priority-sorted list of middleware.
 *
 * This forces non-global middleware to always be in the given order.
 *
 * @var string[]
 */
protected $middlewarePriority = [

    \Illuminate\Foundation\Http\Middleware\HandlePrecognitive
Requests::class,

    \Illuminate\Cookie\Middleware\EncryptCookies::class,

    \Illuminate\Session\Middleware\StartSession::class,

    \Illuminate\View\Middleware\ShareErrorsFromSession::class,

    \Illuminate\Contracts\Auth\Middleware\AuthenticatesRequests::class,

    \Illuminate\Routing\Middleware\ThrottleRequests::class,
```

```
\Illuminate\Routing\Middleware\ThrottleRequestsWithRedis::class,

\Illuminate\Contracts\Session\Middleware\AuthenticatesSessions::-
class,

\Illuminate\Routing\Middleware\SubstituteBindings::class,

\Illuminate\Auth\Middleware\Authorize::class,

];
```

Source: https://laravel.com/docs/

Middleware Parameters

Additionally, middleware can be given more arguments. For instance, you might design an **EnsureUserHasRole** middleware that accepts a role name as a second parameter if your application has to confirm that the authenticated user has a specific "role" before carrying out a specific operation.

After the **$next** argument, the middleware will receive additional parameters:

```php
<?php

namespace App\Http\Middleware;

use Closure;
use Illuminate\Http\Request;
use Symfony\Component\HttpFoundation\Response;

class EnsureEmployeeHasRole
{
    /**
     * Handle an incoming request.
     *
     * @param  \Closure(\Illuminate\Http\Request): (\Symfony\Component\
HttpFoundation\Response)  $next
```

```
    */
    public function handle(Request $request, Closure $next, string
$role): Response
    {
        if (! $request->employee()->hasRole($role)) {


            // Redirect Logic


        }


        return $next($request);
    }


}
```

When specifying the route, middleware parameters may be supplied by separating the middleware name and parameters with a : . Comma-separated lists of arguments should be used:

```
Route::put('/post/{emp_id}', function (string $emp_id) {

    // Code Logic

})->middleware('role:editor')
```

Terminable Middleware

After the HTTP response has been sent to the browser, a middleware may occasionally need to do some tasks. If your middleware contains a **terminate** method and your web server employs FastCGI, the **terminate** method will be automatically invoked following the transmission of the response to the browser:

```
<?php
```

```
namespace Illuminate\Session\Middleware;

use Closure;
use Illuminate\Http\Request;
use Symfony\Component\HttpFoundation\Response;

class TerminatingMiddleware
{

    /**
     * Handle an incoming request.
     *
     * @param  \Closure(\Illuminate\Http\Request): (\Symfony\Component\
HttpFoundation\Response)  $next
     */

    public function handle(Request $request, Closure $next): Response
    {
        return $next($request);
    }

    /**
     * Handle tasks after the response has been sent to the browser.
     */

    public function terminate(Request $request, Response $response):
void
    {
        // Code Logic for termination
    }
}
```

Both the request and the response should be sent to the **terminate** method. Once a terminable middleware has been defined, it should be added to the **app/Http/Kernel.php** file's list of routes or global middleware.

Laravel will resolve a new instance of your middleware from the service container when you use the middleware's **terminate** function. utilize the singleton method of the container to register the middleware if you want to utilize the same instance of the middleware when the **handle** and **terminate** methods are invoked. Normally, this should be carried out in your **AppServiceProvider**'s register method:

```
use App\Http\Middleware\TerminatingMiddleware;


/**
 * Register any application services of the application Logic
 */


public function register(): void
{
    $this->app->singleton(TerminatingMiddleware::class);
}
```

Conclusion

This chapter digs into Laravel's robust authentication system, concentrating on guards, providers, and several authentication techniques. Laravel's authentication system is built on the basic notion of guards and providers.

Authentication and authorization are critical when developing any software application. In the scenario of developing a Laravel application, security, user session management, authorized access, and password management become the critical methods to achieve security in our Laravel application.

Throughout the chapter, we looked into how the same can be achieved with hands-on examples to follow along and it is imperative to have these features in your Laravel application, especially when you will build a multi-user application in Laravel.

In the next chapter, we will look into API development in Laravel, and look into the RSET APIs, the Laravel Passport API, and much more.

Points to Remember

- This chapter digs into Laravel's robust authentication system, concentrating on guards, providers, and several authentication techniques. Laravel's authentication system is built on the basic notion of guards and providers.

- Guards specify each request's authentication mechanism, while providers retrieve users from persistent storage. Laravel has guards such as session guards, which employ cookies and session data to authenticate users.

- The chapter covers the notion of Laravel API Authentication Services, featuring packages such as Passport and Sanctum for handling API tokens and authentication requests. It stresses how these packages work in conjunction with the built-in cookie-based authentication scheme.

- Customization of authentication and registration logic is shown, highlighting HTTP Authentication as a way to quickly authenticate users without requiring a separate login page. API token authentication is illustrated using stateless HTTP Authentication.

- The chapter also goes into bespoke user providers for non-standard relational databases, walking readers through the process of creating and deploying these providers. Laravel's contracts, such as UserProvider and Authenticatable, are well-defined.

- Furthermore, the chapter demonstrates how to invalidate sessions across various devices to ensure user security.

- Remember the functionality, middleware, and authentication routing are all addressed, as well as the construction and use of custom guards. The notion of middleware is investigated, both for route security and for doing activities before or after request processing.

CHAPTER 7

Developing APIs with Laravel

Introduction

This chapter will cover the API development with Laravel. It will teach the user right from introduction on REST APIs to additional complex topics on APIs. The chapter will also focus on Laravel Passport API, its features, and much more.

Structure

In this chapter, we will cover the following topics:

- Understanding APIs, REST
- Resources, Collections and Nesting Relationships
    - Writing Resources
        - Relationships
        - Data Wrapping
        - Pagination
        - Conditional Relationships
    - Resource Response
- Laravel Passport
    - Installation and Setup
    - Configuration
    - Access Tokens
    - Protecting Routes
    - Token Scopes

Understanding APIs, REST

API stands for Application Programming Interface. APIs can be paralleled to a set of protocols between different software programs to communicate with each other, that is, to share data and/or functionality with each other.

There are two types of APIs widely used:

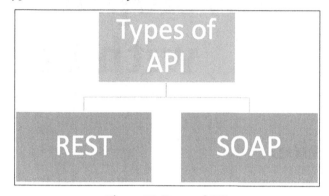

Figure 7.1: Types of API

REST

REST API stands for Representational State Transfer.

It is a single resource for multiple actions in the API layer and uses CRUD (Create, Read, Update, Delete) operations to manipulate and transform data.

SOAP

SOAP API stands for Simple Object Access Protocol.

It can be both stateful and stateless. It makes its calls using POST and also exposes the method calls that are done for communication and transfer of data packets.

Resources, Collections and Nesting Relationships

When establishing the resource instance in your route or controller, you should use the **collection** method offered by your resource class if you are delivering a paginated response or a collection of resources:

```
use App\Http\Resources\UserResource;
use App\Models\User;
```

```
Route::get('/users', function () {
    return UserResource::collection(User::all());

});
```

Please take note that custom metadata additions are not permitted and must be returned with your collection. You may make a specific resource to represent the collection if you would like to alter the resource collection response:

```
php artisan make:resource UserCollection
```

Any metadata that has to be included with the response can be readily defined after the resource collection class has been generated:

```php
<?php

namespace App\Http\Resources;

use Illuminate\Http\Request;
use Illuminate\Http\Resources\Json\ResourceCollection;

class UserCollection extends ResourceCollection
{
    /**
     * Transform the resource collection into an array.
     *
     * @return array<int|string, mixed>
     */
```

```
    public function toArray(Request $request): array
    {
        return [

            'data' => $this->collection,

            'links' => [
                'self' => 'link-value',
            ],

        ];
    }
}
```

Source: www.laravel.com

It might be returned by a route or controller once you have defined your resource collection:

```
use App\Http\Resources\UserCollection;
use App\Models\User;

Route::get('/users', function () {

    return new UserCollection(User::all());

});
```

Laravel restores the resource collection's keys to their numerical order upon returning them from a route. Nonetheless, you may provide a **preserveKeys** attribute in your resource class that indicates if the original keys of a collection need to be kept:

```php
<?php

namespace App\Http\Resources;

use Illuminate\Http\Resources\Json\JsonResource;

class UserResource extends JsonResource
{
    /**
     * Indicates if the resource's collection keys should be preserved.
     *
     * @var bool
     */

    public $preserveKeys = true;
}
```

Collection keys will be kept when the collection is returned from a route or controller if the **preserveKeys** attribute is set to **true**:

```php
use App\Http\Resources\UserResource;
use App\Models\User;

Route::get('/users', function () {

    return UserResource::collection(User::all()->keyBy->id);

});
```

A resource collection's **$this->collection** attribute is usually immediately supplied with the outcome of mapping each item to its unique resource class. Without the trailing **Collection** part in the class name, the single resource class is taken to be the collection's class name. Furthermore, **Resource** may or may not be suffixed to the solitary resource class, based on your personal desire.

UserCollection, for instance, will try to map the supplied user instances to the **UserResource** resource. You may modify this behavior by overriding your resource collection's **$collects** property:

```php
<?php

namespace App\Http\Resources;

use Illuminate\Http\Resources\Json\ResourceCollection;

class UserCollection extends ResourceCollection
{

    public $collects = Member::class;
}
```

Writing Resource

All that is required are resources to convert a given model into an array. Therefore, every resource has a **toArray** function that converts the characteristics of your model into an array that is compatible with APIs and can be obtained by your application's routes or controllers:

```php
<?php

namespace App\Http\Resources;

use Illuminate\Http\Request;
use Illuminate\Http\Resources\Json\JsonResource;

class UserResource extends JsonResource
{
```

```
public function toArray(Request $request): array
{
    return [

        'id' => $this->id,
        'name' => $this->name,
        'city' => $this->city,
        'created_at' => $this->created_at,
        'updated_at' => $this->updated_at,

    ];
}
}
```

A resource can be returned straight from a route or controller after it has been defined:

```
use App\Http\Resources\UserResource;
use App\Models\User;

Route::get('/user/{id}', function (string $id) {

    return new UserResource(User::findOrFail($id));

});
```

Relationships

You can add related resources to the array that your resource's **toArray** function returns if you would like to include them in your answer. In this example, we will add the user's blog posts to the resource response using the **collection** function of the **PostResource** resource:

```php
use App\Http\Resources\PostResource;
use Illuminate\Http\Request;



public function toArray(Request $request): array
{
    return [

        'id' => $this->id,
        'name' => $this->name,
        'city' => $this->city,
        'posts' => PostResource::collection($this->posts),
        'created_at' => $this->created_at,
        'updated_at' => $this->updated_at,


    ];
}
```

Data Wrapping

When the resource response is translated to JSON, your outermost resource is automatically wrapped in a data key. Thus, for instance, the following is a typical resource collection response:

```json
{
    "data": [
        {
            "id": 1,
            "name": "Eladio Schroeder Sr.",
            "city": "NYC"
        },
        {
            "id": 2,
```

```
            "name": "Liliana Mayert",
            "city": "PUNE"
        }
    ]
}
```

Define a **$wrap** property on the resource class if you want to utilize a custom key in place of **data**:

```php
<?php

namespace App\Http\Resources;

use Illuminate\Http\Resources\Json\JsonResource;

class UserResource extends JsonResource
{

    public static $wrap = 'user';
}
```

You should use the **withoutWrapping** method on the base **Illuminate\Http\ Resources\Json\JsonResource** class to eliminate the wrapping of the outermost resource. Generally, for each request made to your application, you should invoke this function from your **AppServiceProvider** or another service provider:

```php
<?php

namespace App\Providers;

use Illuminate\Http\Resources\Json\JsonResource;
use Illuminate\Support\ServiceProvider;

class AppServiceProvider extends ServiceProvider
```

```
{

    public function register(): void
    {

        // Register Logic

    }


    public function boot(): void
    {
        JsonResource::withoutWrapping();
    }
}
```

Understanding Data Wrapping

A Laravel paginator object can be sent to a custom resource collection or the resource collection function of a resource:

```
use App\Http\Resources\UserCollection;
use App\Models\User;


Route::get('/users', function () {

    return new UserCollection(User::paginate());

});
```

Metadata and link keys containing details about the paginator's status are always present in paginated responses:

```
{
    "data": [
        {
            "id": 1,
            "name": "ABC",
            "city": "PUNE"
        },
        {
            "id": 2,
            "name": "PQR",
            "email": "SEATTLE"
        }
    ],
    "links":{
        "first": "http://example.com/users?page=1",
        "last": "http://example.com/users?page=1",
        "prev": null,
        "next": null
    },
    "meta":{
        "current_page": 1,
        "from": 1,
        "last_page": 1,
        "path": "http://example.com/users",
        "per_page": 12,
        "to": 10,
        "total": 10
    }
}
```

You may define a **paginationInformation** method on the resource if you would like to alter the data that appears in the **links** or **meta** keys of the pagination response. The **$paginated** data and the array of **$default** information, which is an array with the **links** and **meta** keys, will be sent to this method:

```
public function paginationInformation($request, $paginated, $default)
{
    $default['links']['custom'] = 'https://example.com';

    return $default;
}
```

Conditional Relationships

You may conditionally include relationships on your resource answers in addition to loading attributes based on whether the connection has previously been loaded on the model. This lets your controller choose which relationships to put into the model, and your resource may conveniently include those relationships only after they have been loaded. In the end, this facilitates avoiding N+1 query issues with your resources.

A relationship can be conditionally loaded using the **whenLoaded** method. This approach accepts the relationship name rather than the connection itself to prevent needlessly loading relationships:

```
use App\Http\Resources\PostResource;



public function toArray(Request $request): array
{
    return [

        'id' => $this->id,
        'name' => $this->name,
        'city' => $this->city,
        'posts' => PostResource::collection($this->whenLoaded('posts')),
        'created_at' => $this->created_at,
```

```
        'updated_at' => $this->updated_at,


    ];
}
```

In this case, the resource response will not be delivered to the client until the posts key has been deleted in the event that the relationship has not loaded.

You may conditionally include relationship *counts* on your resource answers in addition to conditionally include relationships, depending on whether the relationship's count has been loaded into the model:

```
new UserResource($user->loadCount('posts'));
```

You may conditionally include the count of a relationship in your resource response by using the **whenCounted** method. By using this approach, the attribute is not included needlessly if the relationships' count is missing:

```
public function toArray(Request $request): array
{
    return [

        'id' => $this->id,
        'name' => $this->name,
        'city' => $this->city,
        'posts_count' => $this->whenCounted('posts'),
        'created_at' => $this->created_at,
        'updated_at' => $this->updated_at,


    ];
}
```

Resource Response

Routes and controllers have the option of immediately returning resources:

```
use App\Http\Resources\UserResource;
use App\Models\User;

Route::get('/user/{id}', function (string $id) {

    return new UserResource(User::findOrFail($id));

});
```

On occasion, though, you might need to alter the outgoing HTTP response before sending it to the client. To do this, there are two approaches. The response method can be chained onto the resource first. An Illuminate\Http\JsonResponse object will be returned by this function, allowing you complete control over the response's headers:

```
use App\Http\Resources\UserResource;
use App\Models\User;

Route::get('/user', function () {

    return (new UserResource(User::find(1)))

            ->response()

            ->header('X-Value', 'True');

});
```

As an alternative, the resource itself may specify a withResponse method. When the resource is returned in a response as the outermost resource, this procedure will be called:

```php
<?php

namespace App\Http\Resources;

use Illuminate\Http\JsonResponse;
use Illuminate\Http\Request;
use Illuminate\Http\Resources\Json\JsonResource;

class UserResource extends JsonResource
{

    public function toArray(Request $request): array
    {
        return [
            'id' => $this->id,
        ];
    }


    public function withResponse(Request $request, JsonResponse $response): void
    {
        $response->header('the value is', 'True');
    }
}
```

Laravel Passport

For your Laravel application, Laravel Passport offers a complete OAuth2 server solution in a matter of minutes. The League OAuth2 server, which is maintained by Andy Millington and Simon Hamp, provides the foundation upon which Passport is constructed.

Use Laravel Passport if OAuth2 compatibility is a must-have feature for your application.

Installing and Setup

Using the Composer package manager, install Passport:

```
composer require laravel/passport
```

You should migrate your database after installing the package since the service provider for Passport registers its own database migration directory. The tables your application requires to hold OAuth2 clients and access tokens will be created by the Passport migrations:

```
php artisan migrate
```

The `passport:install` Artisan command should then be run. The encryption keys required to produce safe access tokens will be generated by this command. Additionally, *personal access* and *password grant* clients will be created by the command and used to produce access tokens:

```
php artisan passport:install
```

Install the **Laravel\Passport\HasApiTokens** trait to your **App\Models\Employee** model after performing the **passport:install** command. A few assistance methods that let you check the authorized user's token and scopes will be provided by this trait to your model. You may delete the **Laravel\Sanctum\HasApiTokens** trait from your model if it is already using it:

```php
<?php

namespace App\Models;

use Illuminate\Database\Eloquent\Factories\HasFactory;
use Illuminate\Foundation\Auth\User as Authenticatable;
use Illuminate\Notifications\Notifiable;
use Laravel\Passport\HasApiTokens;
```

```
class Employee extends Authenticatable
{
    use HasApiTokens, HasFactory, Notifiable;
}
```

Finally, you need establish an api authentication guard and set the **driver** option to **passport** in your application's **config/auth.php** configuration file. This will tell your program to utilize Passport's **TokenGuard** for incoming API request authentication.

Configuration

To ensure that the secrets of your clients are hashed before being saved in your database, you should invoke the **Passport::hashClientSecrets** function within your **App\Providers\AuthServiceProvider** class' startup method:

```
use Laravel\Passport\Passport;


Passport::hashClientSecrets();
```

All of your client secrets will only be visible to the user as soon as they are created, after they are enabled. If the plain-text client secret value is lost, it cannot be recovered because it is never kept in the database.

Token Lifetimes

Long-lived access tokens that expire after a year are automatically issued by Passport. Use the **tokensExpireIn**, **refreshTokensExpireIn**, and **personalAccessTokensExpireIn** methods to set a longer or shorter token lifespan.

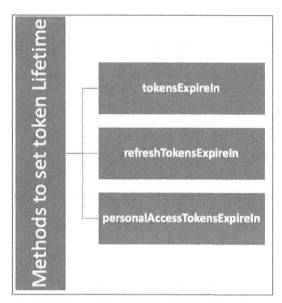

Figure 7.2: *Methods – token lifetime*

The `App\Providers\AuthServiceProvider` class in your application's boot procedure is where these methods should be called:

```
public function boot(): void
{
    Passport::tokensExpireIn(now()->addDays(15));
    Passport::refreshTokensExpireIn(now()->addDays(30));
    Passport::personalAccessTokensExpireIn(now()->addMonths(6));
}
```

Overriding Default Models

By creating your own model and expanding the matching Passport model, you are able to expand the internal models that Passport uses:

```
use Laravel\Passport\Client as PassportClient;

class Client extends PassportClient
{
```

```
    // Code Logic
}
```

Once your model has been defined, you can use the **Laravel\Passport\Passport** class to tell Passport to utilize your custom model. Generally, the **App\Providers\ AuthServiceProvider** class **boot** function in your application is where you should tell Passport about your custom models:

```
use App\Models\Passport\AuthCode;

use App\Models\Passport\Client;

use App\Models\Passport\PersonalAccessClient;

use App\Models\Passport\RefreshToken;

use App\Models\Passport\Token;


public function boot(): void
{
    Passport::useTokenModel(Token::class);

    Passport::useRefreshTokenModel(RefreshToken::class);

    Passport::useAuthCodeModel(AuthCode::class);

    Passport::useClientModel(Client::class);

    Passport::usePersonalAccessClientModel(PersonalAccessClient::class);
}
```

Overriding Routes

There may be occasions when you want to alter the Passport-defined routes. In order to accomplish this, you must first add **Passport::ignoreRoutes** to the **register** function of your application's **AppServiceProvider** in order to ignore the routes registered by Passport:

```
use Laravel\Passport\Passport;


public function register(): void
{
    Passport::ignoreRoutes();
}
```

Next, you may copy and edit the routes that Passport defines in its routes file to the **routes/web.php** file in your application:

```
Route::group([

    'as' => 'passport.',

    'prefix' => config('passport.path', 'oauth'),

    'namespace' => '\Laravel\Passport\Http\Controllers',

], function () {
    // Route Logic
});
```

Access Tokens

OAuth2 is most often known to developers through its use with permission codes. When a client application uses authorization codes, it will send the user to your server, where they can accept or reject the request to provide the client with an access token.

Client

In order to create a communication with your Laravel application, the client is created that enables the communication and interaction with your Laravel application through the application API. In creating a client, the name of the application and the URL of the application are required. The URL is the application URL that an authenticated user will be redirected to.

```
Passport::client Command
```

Using the **passport:client** Artisan command is the most straightforward method of creating a client. You may use this command to make your own clients so you can test the functioning of OAuth2. Passport will ask you for further details about your client when you execute the **client** command and will give you a client ID and secret:

```
php artisan passport:client
```

When asked for the URL by the **passport:client** command, you can enter as many redirect URLs as you'd like for your client by providing a list separated by commas. Every URL that has commas in it has to be URL encoded:

```
http://example1.com/callback
```

```
http://example2.com/callback
```

JSON API

Passport has a JSON API that you may use to create clients, as your application's users won't be able to use the **client** command. By doing this, you may save the hassle of manually coding controllers for client creation, updates, and deletion.

To give your users a dashboard to manage their customers, you must integrate Passport's JSON API with your own frontend. We'll go over each of the API endpoints for client management below. For ease of usage, we will show how to make HTTP queries to the endpoints using Axios.

The **web** and **auth** middleware protect the JSON API, so you can only call it from within your own application. It cannot be invoked by an external source.

GET

```
GET /oauth/clients
```

For the user who has verified their identity, this route returns every client. The main usage for this is to provide a list of all the user's clients, allowing them to be edited or removed:

```
axios.get('/oauth/clients')
    .then(response => {
```

```
        console.log(response.data);
});
```

POST

```
POST /oauth/clients
```

The goal of this route is to attract new customers. A **redirect** URL and the **name** of the customer are the two pieces of information needed. The user will be forwarded to the **redirect** URL when granting or rejecting a permission request.

A client ID and client secret are assigned to it upon creation. When obtaining access tokens from your application, these values will be utilized. The new client instance will be returned by the client creation route:

```
const data = {
    name: 'ABC',
    redirect: 'http://example1.com/callback'
};


axios.post('/oauth/clients', data)
    .then(response => {
        console.log(response.data);
    })
    .catch (response => {
        // Error Handling Logic
    });
```

PUT

```
PUT /oauth/clients/{cliend-id}
```

Client updates are sent over this route. A redirect URL and the **name** of the customer are the two pieces of information needed. The user will be forwarded to the **redirect** URL when granting or rejecting a permission request. The modified client instance will be returned by the route:

```
const data = {
    name: 'ABC',
    redirect: 'http://example1.com/callback'
};


axios.put('/oauth/clients/' + clientId, data)
    .then(response => {
        console.log(response.data);
    })
    .catch (response => {
        // Error Handling Logic
    });
```

DELETE

```
DELETE /oauth/clients/{client-id}


In order to delete clients.


axios.delete('/oauth/clients/' + clientId)
    .then(response => {
        // Code Logic
    });
```

Protecting Routes

The way to ensuring security in the routes is handled in a couple of ways. We will dive into each of them.

Middleware

An authentication guard included into Passport will verify access tokens for incoming requests. You simply need to include the **auth:api** middleware on all routes that need a valid access token after setting up the **api** guard to utilize the **passport** driver:

```
Route::get('/user', function () {
    // Code Logic
})->middleware('auth:api');
```

For each user provider type that your application authenticates—which may involve using completely distinct Eloquent models—you will probably need to specify a guard configuration. By doing this, you may safeguard requests meant for particular user providers. For instance, the **config/auth.php** configuration file has the following guard settings:

```
'api' => [
    'driver' => 'passport',
    'provider' => 'users',
],

'api-customers' => [
    'driver' => 'passport',
    'provider' => 'customers',
],
```

The **api-customers** guard, which verifies incoming requests using the **customers** user provider, will be used in the subsequent route:

```
Route::get('/customer', function () {
    // Code Logic
})->middleware('auth:api-customers');
```

Access Token

Your application's API users should provide their access token as a **Bearer** token in the **Authorization** header of their request when contacting Passport-protected routes. When utilizing the Guzzle HTTP library, for instance:

```
use Illuminate\Support\Facades\Http;


$response = Http::withHeaders([


    'Accept' => 'application/json',
    'Authorization' => 'Bearer '.$accessToken,


])->get('https://passport-app.test/api/user');


return $response->json();
```

Token Scopes

With scopes, your API customers may ask for a certain set of rights when seeking to access an account. For example, not every API customer will want the ability to place orders if you are developing an e-commerce service. Alternatively, you might let customers to see order shipment statuses by only requesting authorization. Put differently, scopes let users of your application restrict what a third-party program may do on their behalf.

Defining a scope

Using the **Passport::tokensCan** function in the boot method of your application's **App\Providers\AuthServiceProvider** class, you may specify the scopes of your API. An array containing scope names and scope descriptions can be used with the **tokensCan** method. Users will see the scope description on the permission approval screen, which may be anything you like to write:

```
public function boot(): void
{
    Passport::tokensCan([
```

```
        'place-alarm' => 'Place alarm',
        'check-weather' => 'Check weather',


    ]);
}
```

Default Scope

You may use the **setDefaultScope** function to configure your Passport server to attach default scope(s) to the token in the event that a client does not request any particular scopes. Usually, you should invoke this function from the **App\ Providers\AuthServiceProvider** class's **boot** method in your application:

```
use Laravel\Passport\Passport;


Passport::tokensCan([
    'place-alarm' => 'Place alarm',
    'check-weather' => 'Check weather',
]);


Passport::setDefaultScope([
    'check-weather',
    'place-alarm',
]);
```

Assign to Tokens

Customers should use the **scope** query string option to indicate the scopes they would want to use when seeking an access token through the authorization code grant. A list of scopes separated by spaces should be the **scope** parameter:

```
Route::get('/redirect', function () {
    $query = http_build_query([
```

```
        'client_id' => 'client-id',

        'redirect_uri' => 'http://example1.com/callback',

        'response_type' => 'code',

        'scope' => 'place-alarm check-weather',


    ]);


    return redirect('http://passport-app.test/oauth/authorize?'.$query);
});
```

The array of desired scopes may be used as the second argument to the **createToken** function of the **App\Models\User** model when providing personal access tokens:

```
$token = $user->createToken('My Token', ['place-alarm'])->accessToken;
```

Check Scope

To confirm that an incoming request is authenticated using a token that has been granted a certain scope, Passport comes with two middleware components. Start by adding the following middleware to your **app/Http/Kernel.php** file's **$middlewareAliases** variable.

```
'scopes' => \Laravel\Passport\Http\Middleware\CheckScopes::class,
```

```
'scope' => \Laravel\Passport\Http\Middleware\CheckForAnyScope::class,
```

To ensure that the incoming request's access token has each of the specified scopes, the scopes middleware may be attached to a route:

```
Route::get('/weather', function () {
```

```
    //Code Logic


})->middleware(['auth:api', 'scopes:check-weather,place-alarm']);
```

In order to confirm that the incoming request's access token has at least one of the specified scopes, the scope middleware may be attached to a route:

```
Route::get('/orders', function () {


    //Code Logic


})->middleware(['auth:api', 'scope:check-weather,place-alarm']);
```

You can still use the **tokenCan** method on the authenticated **App\Models\User** instance to see whether the token has a specified scope after an access token authenticated request has reached your application:

```
use Illuminate\Http\Request;


Route::get('/alarms', function (Request $request) {


    if ($request->user()->tokenCan('place-alarm')) {


        // Code Logic
    }
});
```

Conclusion

An introduction to REST and APIs at the beginning of the chapter emphasizes their importance in the building of contemporary applications. The explanation of resources, collections, and nested connections follows, along with an example of how to use Laravel to put them into practice. Writing resources and maintaining relationships within resource replies are also emphasized in this chapter.

The thorough explanation of Laravel Passport, a comprehensive OAuth2 server solution for Laravel apps, is one of the main features of this chapter. Configuration options for access tokens and token lives are provided, along with a detailed explanation of the installation and setup procedure. Important topics like managing token scopes and safeguarding routes for improved security and access control are also covered in this chapter.

In the next chapter we will look into Testing and Debugging your Laravel Application.

Points to Remember

- Recognize the basics of REST APIs and their importance in the construction of contemporary applications. Use Laravel's hierarchical relationships, collections, and resources to handle data effectively.

- Model data is transformed into an array that is consistent with API replies using Laravel resources.

- It is possible to efficiently maintain relationships between resources in resource answers, which makes it possible to include related resources in the API result. The resource answer is automatically wrapped in a 'data' key in Laravel, but the resource class's $wrap parameter allows you to provide a custom key.

- For a safe and effective OAuth2 server solution, use Laravel Passport. For Laravel apps, Laravel Passport offers a reliable OAuth2 server solution that guarantees safe access to APIs.

- Token scopes are important for giving API users unique access privileges, and there are several ways to handle them in Laravel Passport.

- The client and server may communicate seamlessly by using Laravel Passport to handle JSON APIs and leveraging Axios for HTTP queries.

- Generating encryption keys and establishing clients for API access require a proper installation and configuration of Laravel Passport. To improve security and control over access, set up access tokens and token lives. To provide safe access to important information and features, control token scopes and protect routes.

CHAPTER 8

Testing and Debugging your Laravel Application

Introduction

This chapter covers testing and debugging techniques for Laravel applications. The focus of this chapter is on how to write tests, debug common errors, and use various debugging tools and techniques.

Structure

In this chapter, we will cover the following topics:

- Introduction to Testing in Laravel
- Setting up Environment for Testing
- Testing Lifecycle
    - Creating Tests
    - Running Tests
    - Reporting
    - Profiling
- HTTP Tests
- File Upload Testing
- Debugging in Laravel

Introduction to Testing in Laravel

When it comes to Laravel development, the emphasis is placed on comprehensive testing. The provided `phpunit.xml` file is preconfigured for your application, enabling seamless testing with PHPUnit right from the start. Additionally, the framework includes user-friendly helper functions that facilitate expressive application testing.

For testing Laravel applications, alternative tools like PEST can also be employed.

Within the tests directory of your project, you will find two automatically generated folders: Feature and Unit. Unit tests focus on isolated sections of your code, often targeting a single method. These tests in the `Unit` directory operate independently of your Laravel application's database or other framework services, as they do not boot the application.

On the other hand, Feature tests cover more extensive aspects of your code, including interactions between multiple objects or complete HTTP requests to JSON endpoints. They should constitute the bulk of your testing efforts, offering the highest level of assurance that your system is functioning as intended.

Both the Unit test and Feature test folders contain an `ExampleTest.php` file. Following the installation of a new Laravel application, you can execute your tests using either the `vendor/bin/phpunit` command or the `php artisan test` command.

Setting up Environment for Testing

Laravel autonomously switches the configuration environment to `testing` when tests are executed due to the environment parameters specified within the `phpunit.xml` file. Moreover, during the testing phase, Laravel configures the session and cache to the `array` driver by default, ensuring no persistence of session or cache data.

If you find the need for additional configuration parameters within the `testing` environment, you have the option to create them. You can establish these testing environment variables within your application's `phpunit.xml` file. However, before running your tests, it's crucial to execute the `config:clear` Artisan command in order to clear the configuration cache.

`.env.testing` Environment File

A `.env.testing` file can also be created and placed in the project root. When running PHPUnit tests or using the **--env=testing** option when executing Artisan commands, this file will be utilized in place of the **.env** file.

CreatesApplication Trait

The base **TestCase** class in your application is given the **CreatesApplication** trait that comes with Laravel. The **createApplication** function in this trait bootstraps the Laravel application prior to executing your tests. Certain features, like Laravel's parallel testing functionality, depend on this property, thus it's crucial that you keep it where it was.

Testing Lifecycle

The Testing lifecycle consists of the various steps that should be performed when testing your Laravel Application. The following diagram displays the stages in the Testing Lifecyle for Laravel Applications.

Figure 8.1: *Laravel Application Testing Lifecycle*

Creating Tests

Use the **make:test** Artisan command to generate a new test case. Tests will by default be stored in the **tests/Feature** directory:

```
php artisan make:test SampleTest
```

To create a test within the **tests/Unit** folder directory, use the **-unit** option when executing the **make:test** command:

```
php artisan make:test SampleTest -unit
```

You may provide the make command the **--pest** option if you want to construct a PHP test called **make:test** command:

```
php artisan make:test SampleTest --pest
php artisan make:test SampleTest --unit --pest
```

After the test has been produced, you may use PHPUnit to define test methods as usual. Use the **vendor/bin/phpunit** or **php artisan test** command from your terminal to begin running your tests:

```php
<?php

namespace Tests\Unit;

use PHPUnit\Framework\TestCase;

class Sampletest extends TestCase
{
    public function test_basic_test(): void
    {
        $this->assertTrue(true);

        //Logic of the test case

    }
}
```

Running Tests

In order to run a test, use the phpunit `command`:

```
./vendor/bin/phpunit
```

To run your tests, you can also use the `test` Artisan command in addition to the `phpunit` command. Verbose test results are provided by the Artisan test runner to facilitate development and debugging:

```
php artisan test
```

Any arguments that can be passed to the `phpunit` command may also be passed to the `Artisan test` command:

```
php artisan test --testsuite=Feature --stop-on-failure
```

Parallel Execution of Tests

Typically, PHPUnit and Laravel execute tests sequentially within a single process. Yet, opting for concurrent test execution across multiple processes can substantially reduce the overall testing time. To initiate this process, the initial step involves installing the brianium/paratest Composer package as a `dev` dependency. Subsequently, you can utilize the test Artisan command with the `--parallel` option enabled to implement this approach.

```
composer require brianium/paratest --dev
```

```
php artisan test --parallel
```

Laravel will by default start as many processes as your computer's available CPU cores. However, you may use the `--processes` option to change the number of processes:

```
php artisan test --parallel --processes=2
```

Laravel handles the generation and migration of a test database for each parallel test process, provided a primary database connection has been configured. Each process is assigned a unique process token appended to the test databases. For example, if there are two concurrent test processes, Laravel will create and utilize test databases, including **your_db_test_1** and **your_db_test_2**.

By default, the test databases remain persistent, potentially carrying over data from previous test runs when invoking the **test** Artisan command. However, you can use the **--recreate-databases** option to recreate these databases as needed.

```
php artisan test --parallel --recreate-databases
```

In certain cases, it becomes necessary to configure specific resources for your application's tests, ensuring smooth accessibility for multiple test processes.

Using the **ParallelTesting** facade, you can define code to be executed during the **setUp** and **tearDown** of a process or test case. The specified closures receive the **$token** and **$testCase** variables, which respectively hold the process token and the active test case.

```php
<?php

namespace App\Providers;

use Illuminate\Support\Facades\Artisan;
use Illuminate\Support\Facades\ParallelTesting;
use Illuminate\Support\ServiceProvider;
use PHPUnit\Framework\TestCase;

class AppServiceProvider extends ServiceProvider
{

    public function boot(): void
    {
        ParallelTesting::setUpProcess(function (int $token) {
```

```
        // Set Up Logic


    });


        ParallelTesting::setUpTestCase(function (int $token, TestCase
$testCase) {

        // Set Up Case Logic


    });




        ParallelTesting::setUpTestDatabase(function (string $database,
int $token) {
        Artisan::call('db:seed');

        // Logic


    });


        ParallelTesting::tearDownTestCase(function (int $token, TestCase
$testCase) {

        // Tear Down Logic


    });


        ParallelTesting::tearDownProcess(function (int $token) {

        // Tear Down Process Logic


    });
```

```
    }
}
```

Use the token method to retrieve the current parallel process token from different places in the test code of your application. The allocation of resources across concurrent test processes is made possible by this different string identification that is exclusive to each test process. Laravel, for instance, automatically appends this token to the end of the test databases that are produced by each testing process running in parallel.

```
$token = ParallelTesting::token();
```

Reporting

You might wish to check how much application code is utilized in your tests and whether your test cases truly cover the application code when you run your application tests. You may use the **--coverage** option in conjunction with the **test** command to achieve this:

```
php artisan test --coverage
```

To provide a minimal test coverage criterion for your application, use the **--min** option. If this threshold is not reached, the test suite will fail:

```
php artisan test --coverage --min=80.3
```

Profiling

One handy feature of the Artisan test runner is a way to get a list of the tests that take the longest in your application. To get a list of your 10 slowest tests, run the **test** command with the **--profile** option. This can help you quickly determine which tests need to be modified in order to speed up your test suite:

```
php artisan test --profile
```

HTTP Tests

A very smooth API is offered by Laravel for sending HTTP queries to your application and receiving the results. Consider the feature test described here, for instance:

```php
<?php

namespace Tests\Feature;

use Tests\TestCase;

class ExampleTest extends TestCase
{

    public function test_the_application_returns_a_successful_
response(): void
    {
        $response = $this->get('/');

        $response->assertStatus(200);
    }
}
```

While the **assertStatus** function states that the returned answer should have the specified HTTP status code, the **get** method sends a **GET** request to the application. Laravel has a number of assertions for examining the response headers, content, JSON format, and other elements in addition to this straightforward one.

Make a Request

You may use the get, post, put, patch, or delete methods in your test to send a request to your application. These techniques don't really send your application a *real* HTTP request. Rather, the complete network request is internally emulated.

Test request methods return an instance of **Illuminate\Http\Response** rather than an **Illuminate\Testing\TestResponse** instance, which offers a number of useful assertions that let you investigate the answers of your application:

```php
<?php

namespace Tests\Feature;

use Tests\TestCase;

class ExampleTest extends TestCase
{

    public function basicRequest(): void
    {
        $response = $this->get('/');

        $response->assertStatus(200);
    }
}
```

Generally speaking, there should only be one request made to your application by each test. If a test method is used to run several requests, unexpected behavior could happen.

Customizing Request Headers

Before the request is delivered to the application, you can alter its headers using the **withHeaders** function. You may add any custom headers to the request using this method:

```php
<?php

namespace Tests\Feature;
```

```php
use Tests\TestCase;

class ExampleTest extends TestCase
{

    public function exampleSample(): void
    {
        $response = $this->withHeaders([

            'X-Header' => 'Value',

        ])->post('/user', ['name' => 'ABC']);

        $response->assertStatus(201);
    }
}
```

Cookies

To set cookie values before sending a request, use the **withCookie** or **withCookies** methods. While the **withCookies** function takes an array of name/value pairs as its two parameters, the **withCookie** method accepts a cookie name and value:

```php
<?php

namespace Tests\Feature;

use Tests\TestCase;

class ExampleTest extends TestCase
{
    public function exampleFunctionCookies(): void
    {
        $response = $this->withCookie('color', 'red')->get('/');
```

```php
        $response = $this->withCookies([

            'color' => 'red',
            'name' => 'ABC',

        ])->get('/');
    }
}
```

Authentication

During HTTP testing, Laravel offers a number of utilities for dealing with the session. Using the `withSession` method, you may first assign the session data to a specified array. You may use this to load data into the session before sending a request to your application:

```php
<?php

namespace Tests\Feature;

use Tests\TestCase;

class ExampleTest extends TestCase
{
    public function exampleSessionInteraction(): void
    {

        $response = $this->withSession(['banned' => false])->get('/');

    }
}
```

Usually, state is maintained for the present authorized user using Laravel's session. As a result, the **actingAs** helper function offers a quick and easy manner of confirming that a certain user is the current user. For instance, to create and authenticate a user, we may use a model factory:

```php
<?php

namespace Tests\Feature;

use App\Models\User;
use Tests\TestCase;

class ExampleTest extends TestCase
{

    public function exampleAuth(): void
    {
        $user = User::factory()->create();

        $response = $this->actingAs($user)

                        ->withSession(['banned' => false])

                        ->get('/');
    }

}
```

You can specify the desired guard for user authentication by including the guard name as the second parameter in the **actingAs** function. Throughout the test, the guard assigned to the **actingAs** method will also function as the default guard.

```php
$this->actingAs($user, 'web')
```

Debugging Responses

The **dump**, **dumpHeaders**, and **dumpSession** methods can be used to inspect and debug the response content after submitting a test request to your application.

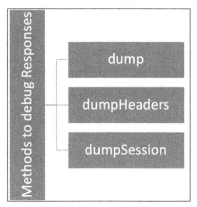

Figure 8.2: *Methods of debugging response*

Let's look at an example:

```php
<?php

namespace Tests\Feature;

use Tests\TestCase;

class ExampleTest extends TestCase
{

    public function exampleTest(): void
    {
        $response = $this->get('/');

        $response->dumpHeaders();

        $response->dumpSession();
```

```
            $response->dump();


    }


}
```

As an alternative, you may suspend execution and dump response-related data using the dd, ddHeaders, and ddSession methods:

```php
<?php

namespace Tests\Feature;

use Tests\TestCase;

class ExampleTest extends TestCase
{

    public function exampleTest(): void
    {
        $response = $this->get('/');

        $response->ddHeaders();

        $response->ddSession();

        $response->dd();

    }

}
```

Exception Handling

At times, it may be necessary to confirm whether a specific exception is being raised within your application. To ensure that the exception is not intercepted by Laravel's exception handler and presented as an HTTP response, you can employ the **withoutExceptionHandling** function before sending your request.

```
$response = $this->withoutExceptionHandling()->get('/');
```

Furthermore, before sending your request, you have the option to utilize the **withoutDeprecationHandling** function, which ensures that your application does not rely on any functionalities that the PHP language or its associated libraries have deprecated. Disabling deprecation handling will result in the transformation of deprecation warnings into exceptions, causing your test to fail.

```
$response = $this->withoutDeprecationHandling()->get('/');
```

To assert that code inside a given closure throws an exception of the designated type, use the **assertThrows** method:

```
$this->assertThrows(

    fn () => (new ProcessOrder)->execute(),

    OrderInvalid::class

);
```

File Upload Testing

For the purpose of testing, you can employ the **fake** function from the **Illuminate\Http\UploadedFile** class to generate mock files or images. This simplifies the testing of file uploads, particularly when used alongside the **Storage** facade's **fake** method. For instance, you can swiftly test an avatar upload form by combining these two functionalities:

```php
<?php

namespace Tests\Feature;

use Illuminate\Http\UploadedFile;
use Illuminate\Support\Facades\Storage;
use Tests\TestCase;

class ExampleTest extends TestCase
{
    public function testUpload(): void
    {
        Storage::fake('cat');

        $file = UploadedFile::fake()->image('cat.jpg');

        $response = $this->post('/cat', [

            'cat' => $file,

        ]);

        Storage::disk('cats')->assertExists($file->hashName());
    }

}
```

You may use the **assertMissing** function offered by the **Storage** facade to assert that a certain file does not exist:

```
Storage::fake('cats');

// Application Logic

Storage::disk('cats')->assertMissing('missing.jpg');
```

To properly test your application's validation requirements, you may provide the width, height, and size of the picture (in kilobytes) when generating files using the **fake** method offered by the **UploadedFile** class:

```
UploadedFile::fake()->image('cat.jpg', $width, $height)->size(100);
```

The **create** method may be used to produce any other sort of file in addition to images:

```
UploadedFile::fake()->create('document.pdf', $sizeInKilobytes);
```

If necessary, you may specify the MIME type that the file should return directly by passing a **$mimeType** parameter to the method:

```
UploadedFile::fake()->create(

    'document.pdf', $sizeInKilobytes, 'application/pdf'

);
```

Debugging in Laravel

Using Xdebug for step debugging is supported by Homestead. For instance, PHP will establish a connection with your IDE when you open a page in your browser, enabling you to view and edit the code that is now running.

Xdebug is launched and ready to receive connections by default. Use the **sudo phpenmod xdebug** command in your Homestead virtual machine if you need to activate Xdebug on the CLI. Now enable debugging by following the instructions in your IDE. Lastly, set up your browser such that a bookmarklet or extension will launch Xdebug.

It is easier to autostart debugging functional tests that send queries to the web server than it is to change the tests such that debugging is triggered by passing via a special header or cookie. In your Homestead virtual machine, edit the **/etc/php/7.x/fpm/conf.d/20-xdebug.ini** file and add the following settings to have Xdebug launch automatically:

```
xdebug.client_host = 192.168.10.1
xdebug.mode = debug
xdebug.start_with_request = yes
```

Use the xphp shell alias on your Homestead virtual machine to debug a PHP CLI application:

```
xphp /path/to/script
```

Conclusion

In this chapter, we covered the essential aspects of testing and debugging your Laravel application. The chapter begins by introducing the testing features of Laravel, including the preconfigured phpunit.xml file and the helper functions that facilitate testing. It discusses the testing structure, including the Feature and Unit test folders, and emphasizes the importance of testing different aspects of the application. The chapter delves into the setup environment for testing, the **.env.testing** file, and the **CreatesApplication** trait.

The chapter explains the testing lifecycle in Laravel, covering the creation and execution of tests, reporting, profiling, and parallel execution. It discusses HTTP testing, including making requests, customizing headers, dealing with cookies, and authentication. Furthermore, it provides insights into debugging responses, handling exceptions, and testing file uploads. The chapter concludes by explaining how to use Xdebug for step debugging in the Laravel Homestead environment.

Throughout the chapter, various code examples and practical tips are provided to help readers understand and implement testing and debugging techniques effectively in their Laravel applications. The chapter aims to equip developers with the necessary knowledge and tools to create robust and well-tested Laravel applications.

In the next chapter, we will be looking at the mail and notifications feature of Laravel that provides this feature to the APIs.

Points to Remember

- Testing a Laravel application involves a structured approach, distinguishing between Unit and Feature tests. Unit tests focus on isolated code segments, evaluating individual functions, while Feature tests explore the interactions among components, including complex dynamics and HTTP request assessments. Emphasizing comprehensive testing across various application facets ensures a robust codebase. Configuring the testing environment is critical, involving adjustments in the phpunit.xml file and utilizing the .env.testing file for specific testing configurations. The CreatesApplication trait aids in seamless Laravel application bootstrapping before testing, ensuring a smooth experience.

- Understanding the testing lifecycle is essential, encompassing test creation, execution, reporting, and profiling. Efficient parallel execution reduces testing time, optimizing the testing process. HTTP testing in Laravel involves powerful tools for querying applications and authenticating users, requiring mastery of header customization, cookie setting, session management, and user authentication. Debugging techniques involve tools like dump, dd, and Xdebug in Laravel Homestead for step debugging. File upload testing demands scrutiny of the UploadedFile class and Storage facade functionalities, ensuring rigorous validation and system integrity.

- Adhering to best practices, such as minimal test coverage enforcement and application profiling, guarantees a reliable codebase. Consistent environment configuration across testing stages is crucial to avoid discrepancies, facilitating efficient transitions. Collaboration and open communication among team members enhance testing and debugging execution, with comprehensive documentation serving as a valuable knowledge-sharing resource, fostering continuous learning within the team.

## CHAPTER 9

E-mail and Notifications in Laravel

Introduction

The chapter focuses on e-mail and notifications feature of Laravel that provides this feature to the APIs. Notifications provide an excellent way to monitor, receive alerts and evaluate the performance of the Laravel application.

Structure

In this chapter, we will cover the following topics:

- Generating Notifications
- Sending Notifications
  - Delivery Channels
  - Queuing Notifications
  - Delaying Notifications
  - Custom Notification Queue
  - Custom Notification Channel Queue
  - On-Demand Notifications
- Mail Notifications
  - Customizing Email Components
  - Custom templates

-      o   Handling Raw Data
-      o   Tags and Metadata
-      o   Custom Symfony Message
- Broadcast Notifications
- Notification Events

Generating Notifications

A single class, usually kept in the **app/Notifications** directory, represents each notification in Laravel. When you use the **make:notification** command in your program, this directory will be generated in the application:

```
php artisan make:notification orderRecieved
```

A new notification class will be added to your **app/Notifications** directory by using this command. A **via** method and a variety of message building methods, such as **toMail** or **toDatabase**, that transform the notification into a message specific to that channel are included in every notification class.

Sending Notifications

Notifications can be issued using the **Notification** facade or the **notify** method of the **Notifiable** trait. By default, the **App\Models\User** model in your application has the Notifiable trait included:

```php
<?php

namespace App\Models;

use Illuminate\Foundation\Auth\User as Authenticatable;
use Illuminate\Notifications\Notifiable;

class User extends Authenticatable
{
```

```
    use Notifiable;


}
```

This trait's notify function anticipates receiving the following notification instance:

```
use App\Notifications\orderRecieved;


$user->notify(new orderRecieved($order));
```

An effective way to dispatch notifications to multiple notifiable entities is by leveraging the **Notification** facade. By invoking the **send** function and providing the notification object alongside the relevant notifiable entities, you can conveniently deliver notifications to a group of users or recipients.

```
use Illuminate\Support\Facades\Notification;


Notification::send($users, new orderRecieved($order));
```

You may use the **sendNow** method to send notifications right away as well. Even if the notification implements the **ShouldQueue** interface, this method will send the notice right away:

```
Notification::sendNow($developers, new DeploymentCompleted($deployment));
```

Delivery Channels

Each notification class contains a via method that determines the specific channels through which the notification will be dispatched. Various channels such as **mail**, **database**, **broadcast**, **Vonage**, and **Slack** can be utilized for sending notifications.

A **$notifiable** instance—an instance of the class to which the notification is being sent—is received by the via method. To choose which channels the notice should be sent on, use **$notifiable**:

```php
public function via(object $notifiable): array
{

    return $notifiable->prefers_sms ? ['vonage'] : ['mail', 'database'];

}
```

Queuing Notifications

Notification delivery can be slow, particularly if the channel has to use an external API to provide the message. Allow your notification to be queued by including the **ShouldQueue** interface and **Queueable** trait in your class to improve the response time of your application. You may add the interface and trait to your notification class right away because they are already imported for all notifications created with the **make:notification** command:

```php
<?php

namespace App\Notifications;

use Illuminate\Bus\Queueable;
use Illuminate\Contracts\Queue\ShouldQueue;
use Illuminate\Notifications\Notification;

class orderRecieved extends Notification implements ShouldQueue
{
    use Queueable;

    // Logic
}
```

After your notice has been updated with the **ShouldQueue** interface, you may send it normally. When a class has the **ShouldQueue** interface, Laravel will recognize it and queue up the notification delivery automatically:

```
$user->notify(new orderRecieved($invoice));
```

Every recipient and channel combination will result in the creation of a queued job when queueing notifications. For instance, if your notice includes two channels and three receivers, six jobs will be added to the queue.

Delaying Notifications

You may link the **delay** method onto your notification instantiation to postpone the notice's delivery:

```
$delay = now()->addMinutes(10);

$user->notify((new orderRecieved($invoice))->delay($delay));
```

The **delay** function allows you to supply an array to set the delay amount for each channels:

```
$user->notify((new orderRecieved($invoice))->delay([

    'mail' => now()->addMinutes(2),
    'sms' => now()->addMinutes(5),

]));
```

As an alternative, the notification class itself may define a **withDelay** method. Channel names and delay values should be returned as an array by the **withDelay** method:

```
public function withDelay(object $notifiable): array
{

    return [
        'mail' => now()->addMinutes(2),
        'sms' => now()->addMinutes(5),
    ];

}
```

Custom Notification Queue

Queued alerts will be automatically queued over the default queue connection of your application. You may call the **onConnection** function from your notification's constructor if you want to choose a different connection to be utilized for a certain notification:

```
<?php

namespace App\Notifications;

use Illuminate\Bus\Queueable;
use Illuminate\Contracts\Queue\ShouldQueue;
use Illuminate\Notifications\Notification;

class orderRecieved extends Notification implements ShouldQueue
{
    use Queueable;


    public function __construct()
    {
```

```
        $this->onConnection('redis');


    }


}
```

Alternatively, you may define a **viaConnections** function on your notification to indicate which queue connection should be utilized for each notification channel that the notification supports. An array of channel name / queue connection name pairs ought to be the result of this method:

```
public function viaConnections(): array
{
    return [
        'mail' => 'redis',
        'database' => 'sync',
    ];
}
```

Custom Notification Channel Queue

You may define a **viaQueues** method on your notification to indicate which queue should be utilized for each notification channel that the notification supports. An array of channel name / queue name pairs ought to be the result of this method:

```
public function viaQueues(): array
{
    return [

        'mail' => 'mail-queue',
        'slack' => 'slack-queue',

    ];
}
```

When queued alerts are sent within database transactions, the queue may handle them before the database transaction commits. Any adjustments you make to models or database records during the database transaction may not yet be reflected in the database if this occurs. Furthermore, any models or database entries produced during the transaction may no longer exist in the database. If your notification is based on these models, unanticipated problems may arise during the processing of the task that sends the queued notice.

If the **after_commit** configuration option for your queue connection is set to **false**, you may still specify that a specific queued notification be dispatched after all open database transactions have been committed by utilizing the **afterCommit** method when delivering the notification:

```php
use App\Notifications\orderRecieved;
```

```php
$user->notify((new orderRecieved($order))->afterCommit());
```

Or call the afterCommit method from constructor of notification.

```php
<?php

namespace App\Notifications;

use Illuminate\Bus\Queueable;
use Illuminate\Contracts\Queue\ShouldQueue;
use Illuminate\Notifications\Notification;

class orderRecieved extends Notification implements ShouldQueue
{
    use Queueable;

    public function __construct()
    {
        $this->afterCommit();
```

```
        }
}
```

After a queued notification is dispatched for background processing, it is normally received by a queue worker and delivered to its designated receiver.

If you want to make the ultimate decision on whether to send a queued notification after it has been processed by a queue worker, you may specify a **shouldSend** method on the notification class. The notice will not be delivered if this method returns **false**:

```
public function shouldSend(object $notifiable, string $channel): bool
{
    return $this->order->isMade();
}
```

On-Demand Notifications

You may need to send a notice to someone who is not registered as a user of your program on occasion. Before delivering the message, you may supply ad-hoc notification routing information using the message facade's **route** method:

```
use Illuminate\Broadcasting\Channel;
use Illuminate\Support\Facades\Notification;

Notification::route('mail', 'abc@example.com')
            ->route('vonage', '5555555555')
            ->route('slack', '#slack-new')
            ->route('broadcast', [new Channel('channel-name')])
            ->notify(new orderRecieved($order));
```

If you want to include the recipient's name while sending an on-demand notice to the mail route, use an array with the email address as the key and the name as the value of the first element:

```
Notification::route('mail', [

    'qwerty@example.com' => 'Sample Name',

])->notify(new orderRecieved($order));
```

Mail Notifications

If a notice can be sent as an email, the notification class should include a **toMail** function. This function should return an **IlluminateNotificationsMessagesMail Message** instance after receiving a **$notifiable** entity.

The **MailMessage** class has a few simple methods for creating transactional email messages. Lines of text and a call to action can be included in email communications. Let's look at an example of the **toMail** method:

```
public function toMail(object $notifiable): MailMessage
{
    $url = url('/order/'.$this->invoice->id);

    return (new MailMessage)
                ->greeting('Hello!')
                ->line('We have recieved your order')
                ->lineIf($this->amount > 0, "Amount paid: {$this-
>amount}")
                ->action('View Bill', $url)
                ->line('Thank you for using our application!');
}
```

In this example, we have a welcome, a line of text, a call to action, and another line of text. The **MailMessage** object's methods make it simple and quick to prepare tiny transactional emails. The message components will subsequently be translated by the mail channel into a beautiful, responsive HTML email design with a plain-text equivalent.

Instead of setting the *lines* of text in the notification class, you may use the view function to define a custom template for rendering the notification email:

```php
public function toMail(object $notifiable): MailMessage
{
    return (new MailMessage)->view(

        'emails.name', ['order' => $this->order]

    );
}
```

You may define a plain-text view for the mail message by supplying the view name to the **view** method as the second member of an array:

```php
public function toMail(object $notifiable): MailMessage
{
    return (new MailMessage)->view(

        ['emails.name.html', 'emails.name.plain'],
        ['order' => $this->order]

    );
}
```

Customizing Email Components

The sender / from address of emails is set by default in the **config/mail.php** configuration file. However, you may use the **from** method to provide the from address for a single notification:

```php
public function toMail(object $notifiable): MailMessage
{
```

```php
    return (new MailMessage)
                ->from('abc@example.com', 'Sample Name')
                ->line('...');
}
```

The notification system will automatically check for an **email** attribute on your notifiable object when sending alerts over the **mail** channel. By establishing a **routeNotificationForMail** method on the notifiable entity, you may specify which email address is used to deliver the notification:

```php
<?php

namespace App\Models;

use Illuminate\Foundation\Auth\User as Authenticatable;
use Illuminate\Notifications\Notifiable;
use Illuminate\Notifications\Notification;

class User extends Authenticatable
{
    use Notifiable;

    public function routeNotificationForMail(Notification $notification):
array|string
    {

        // Return email address
        return $this->email_address;

        // Return email address and name
        return [$this->email_address => $this->name];


    }
}
```

The topic of the email is the class name of the notice formatted to *Title Case* by default. So, if your notification class is called **orderComplete**, the topic of the email will be **orderComplete**. If you want to specify a different **subject** for the message, use the subject method when creating the message:

```
public function toMail(object $notifiable): MailMessage
{
    return (new MailMessage)
                ->subject('Notification Subject')
                ->line('...');
}
```

The email notice is delivered by default using the default mailer set in the config/mail.php configuration file. However, you may change the mailer at runtime by invoking the mailer function when creating your message:

```
public function toMail(object $notifiable): MailMessage
{
    return (new MailMessage)
                ->mailer('postmark')
                ->line('...');
}
```

Custom templates

By exposing the notification package's resources, you may edit the HTML and plain-text templates used by mail notifications. The mail notification templates will be located in the **resources/views/vendor/notifications** directory once you execute this command:

```
php artisan vendor:publish --tag=laravel-notifications
```

When creating an email notice, utilize the **attach** method to include attachments. As its first parameter, the **attach** method accepts the absolute path to the file:

```
public function toMail(object $notifiable): MailMessage
{
    return (new MailMessage)
                ->greeting(Welcome!')
                ->attach('/path/to/file');
}
```

You may define the display name and/or MIME type when adding files to a message by giving an **array** as the second argument to the **attach** method:

```
public function toMail(object $notifiable): MailMessage
{

    return (new MailMessage)

                ->greeting('Welcome!')

                ->attach('/path/to/file', [

                    'as' => 'name.pdf',

                    'mime' => 'application/pdf',

                ]);

}
```

Unlike attaching files in mailable objects, **attachFromStorage** does not allow you to **attach** a file straight from a storage drive. Use the attach method with an absolute path to the file on the storage drive instead. Alternatively, you might use the **toMail** function to return a mailable:

```
use App\Mail\InvoicePaid as OrderRecievedMailable;


public function toMail(object $notifiable): Mailable
{
    return (new OrderRecievedMailable($this->order))


            ->to($notifiable->email)


            ->attachFromStorage('/path/to/file');
}
```

Multiple files can be connected to a message using the **attachMany** function when necessary:

```
public function toMail(object $notifiable): MailMessage
{
    return (new MailMessage)
                ->greeting('Welcome!')
                ->attachMany([
                    '/path/to/forge.svg',
                    '/path/to/vapor.svg' => [
                        'as' => 'Logo1.svg',
                        'mime' => 'image/svg+xml',
                    ],
                ]);
}
```

Handling Raw Data

Attach a raw string of bytes as an attachment using the **attachData** function. When invoking the **attachData** function, give the filename to be allocated to the attachment:

```php
public function toMail(object $notifiable): MailMessage
{
    return (new MailMessage)

                ->greeting('Welcome!')

                ->attachData($this->pdf, 'name.pdf', [

                    'mime' => 'application/pdf',

                ]);
}
```

Tags and Metadata

Message *tags* and *metadata* are supported by certain third-party email providers, such as Mailgun and Postmark, and may be used to organize and monitor emails sent by your application. Tags and metadata can be added to an email message using the **tag** and **metadata** methods:

```php
public function toMail(object $notifiable): MailMessage
{
    return (new MailMessage)

                ->greeting('Upvoted!')

                ->tag('upvote')

                ->metadata('comment_id', $this->comment->id);
}
```

If your application is utilizing the Mailgun driver, you may find additional information about tags and metadata in Mailgun's documentation. Similarly, the Postmark documentation may be reviewed for further information on their tag and metadata capabilities.

If your application sends emails over Amazon SES, you should utilize the `metadata` approach to attach SES tags to the message.

Custom Symfony Message

The `MailMessage` class's `withSymfonyMessage` function allows you to register a closure that will be executed with the Symfony Message instance before sending the message. This allows you to fully tweak the message before it is delivered:

```
use Symfony\Component\Mime\Email;

public function toMail(object $notifiable): MailMessage
{
    return (new MailMessage)

            ->withSymfonyMessage(function (Email $message) {

                $message->getHeaders()->addTextHeader(

                    'Custom-Header', 'Header Value'

                );
            });
}
```

Broadcast Notifications

The `broadcast` channel uses Laravel's event broadcasting services to send alerts, allowing your JavaScript-powered frontend to receive them in real-time. If a notification allows broadcasting, a `toBroadcast` function on the notification class can be defined. This function takes a `$notifiable` entity and returns a

BroadcastMessage instance. If the **toBroadcast** method does not exist, the data that should be broadcast will be gathered using the **toArray** method. The data received will be encoded as JSON and sent to your JavaScript-powered frontend. Let's look at an example of the Broadcast method:

```
use Illuminate\Notifications\Messages\BroadcastMessage;

public function toBroadcast(object $notifiable): BroadcastMessage
{
    return new BroadcastMessage([

        'order_id' => $this->order->id,

        'amount' => $this->order->amount,

    ]);

}
```

All broadcast alerts have been queued for transmission. You may utilize the **onConnection** and **onQueue** methods of the **BroadcastMessage** to configure the queue connection or queue name that is used to queue the broadcast operation:

```
return (new BroadcastMessage($data))
                ->onConnection('sqs')
                ->onQueue('broadcasts');
```

In addition to the data you supply, all broadcast notifications feature a **type** field that contains the notification's complete class name. If you want to change the notification **type**, add a **broadcastType** function on the notification class:

```
public function broadcastType(): string
{
    return 'broadcast.message';
```

```
}
```

Notifications will be broadcast on a private channel using the **notifiable.id** convention. As a result, if you send a notice to an **App\Models\User** instance with an ID of 1, it will be broadcast on the **App.Models.User**. There is just one private channel. You can simply listen for alerts on a channel while using Laravel Echo by utilizing the **notification** method:

```
Echo.private('App.Models.User.' + userId)
    .notification((notification) => {
        console.log(notification.type);
    });
```

You may implement a **receivesBroadcastNotificationsOn** method on the notifiable entity to control which channel an entity's broadcast notifications are broadcast on:

```php
<?php

namespace App\Models;

use Illuminate\Broadcasting\PrivateChannel;
use Illuminate\Foundation\Auth\User as Authenticatable;
use Illuminate\Notifications\Notifiable;

class User extends Authenticatable
{
    use Notifiable;

    public function receivesBroadcastNotificationsOn(): string
    {

        return 'users.'.$this->id;
```

```
    }
}
```

Notification Events

The notification system dispatches the `Illuminate\Notifications\Events\`
`NotificationSending` event when a notification is sent. This holds the *notifiable*
object as well as the notification instance. Listeners for this event can be
registered in your application's `EventServiceProvider`:

```
use App\Listeners\CheckNotificationStatus;
use Illuminate\Notifications\Events\NotificationSending;

protected $listen = [

    NotificationSending::class => [

        CheckNotificationStatus::class,

    ],

];
```

If an event listener for the `NotificationSending` event returns `false` from its
`handle` function, the notice will not be sent:

```
use Illuminate\Notifications\Events\NotificationSending;

public function handle(NotificationSending $event): bool
{
    return false;
}
```

You may discover more about the notification recipient or the notification itself by accessing the event's notifiable, notification, and channel attributes from inside an event listener:

```
public function handle(NotificationSending $event): void
{
    // $event->channel
    // $event->notifiable
    // $event->notification
}
```

When a notice is sent, the **IlluminateNotificationsEventsNotification** object is created. The notification system sends out the sent event. This holds the *notifiable* object as well as the notification instance. Listeners for this event can be registered in your `EventServiceProvider`:

```
use App\Listeners\LogNotification;
use Illuminate\Notifications\Events\NotificationSent;


protected $listen = [

    NotificationSent::class => [

        LogNotification::class,

    ],
];
```

To discover more about the notification recipient or the notification itself, you may use an event listener to obtain the event's notifiable, notification, channel, and response properties:

```
public function handle(NotificationSent $event): void
{
    // $event->channel
    // $event->notifiable
    // $event->notification
    // $event->response
}
```

Conclusion

In this chapter, we delved into the crucial aspects of leveraging e-mail and notifications in Laravel, highlighting its usefulness in tracking application performance and enabling effective communication with users. The chapter outlines the key functionalities and processes involved in incorporating this feature within the Laravel framework.

The chapter is structured into distinct sections, covering the generation and dispatching of notifications, various delivery channels, queuing and delaying notifications, as well as customizing the notification queue and channel. Additionally, it addresses the utilization of on-demand notifications, mail notifications, and the customization of email components through custom templates, handling raw data, and incorporating tags and metadata. The chapter also discusses broadcast notifications and the essential considerations associated with notification events, providing valuable insights into their integration within the Laravel ecosystem.

By offering a comprehensive overview of the nuances and intricacies involved in implementing e-mail and notification functionalities, this chapter equips developers with a deeper understanding of how to effectively utilize these features within their Laravel applications. The practical insights provided throughout the chapter empower developers to create robust and efficient notification systems that enhance user engagement and interaction.

In the next chapter, we will learn how to deploy our Laravel application to the cloud using cloud platform.

Points to Remember

- Notifications in Laravel are represented by a single class, with each notification having various methods like `toMail` or toDatabase to transform the notification into specific message formats for different channels.

- Notifications can be sent using the Notification facade or the notify method of the Notifiable trait. You can send notifications to multiple notifiable entities using the send function.

- Laravel supports various delivery channels, such as mail, database, broadcast, Vonage, and Slack. You can determine the channels a notification should be sent through by using the $notifiable instance.

- By implementing the `ShouldQueue` interface and Queueable trait, notifications can be queued for improved application response time. The `sendNow` method sends notifications immediately, even if they implement the `ShouldQueue` interface.

- Notifications can be delayed using the delay method, allowing you to set specific times for notification delivery. You can set different delay times for different channels as well.

- You can choose a specific queue connection for notifications by using the `onConnection` function. Additionally, you can define the queue connection for each notification channel using the `viaConnections` method.

- You can specify the queue for each notification channel using the `viaQueues` method. Be aware of potential conflicts between database transactions and queued notifications.

- Using the route method from the message facade, you can send notifications to recipients not registered as users in your application, providing ad-hoc notification routing information.

- Customize the email components using the `toMail` function, allowing you to define the structure of the email content. You can also customize the sender's address and utilize custom email templates for rendering notifications.

- Leverage the view method to define custom templates for rendering notification emails, enabling the creation of personalized and visually appealing email notifications.

- Use the `attachData` and attach methods to include attachments or raw data in email notifications, enhancing the informational value and interactivity of the emails.

- Implement tags and metadata in the email message to organize and monitor the emails sent by the application, providing additional context and information for tracking and management purposes.

- Use the `withSymfonyMessage` function to fully customize the message before sending it, allowing for more granular control over the content and structure of the email message.

- Implement the `toBroadcast` function to send notifications over Laravel's event broadcasting services, enabling real-time communication with JavaScript-powered frontends.

- Utilize the `NotificationSending` and `NotificationSent` events to monitor and manage notification activities, providing an opportunity to intervene or gather additional information during the notification sending process.

## CHAPTER 10

Deploying your Laravel App to Cloud

Introduction

In this chapter, we will learn how to deploy our Laravel application to the cloud using cloud platform. We will cover the necessary steps and configurations to deploy our app on cloud infrastructure, including cloud server setup, setting up environment variables, uploading files, and creating databases. This chapter covers Laravel Vapor in depth and uses references from the documentation at `docs.vapor.build.`

Structure

We will cover the following topics in this chapter:

- Cloud Deployment Fundamentals
- Cloud Providers Overview
  - Heroku
  - AWS
  - Google Cloud
- Laravel Application Deployment with Vapor
  - Installation
  - Environment
  - Deployment

- o Development
- o Domains
- Troubleshooting

Cloud Deployment Fundamentals

The use of the cloud is critical to the effective and scalable functioning of Laravel applications. There are various benefits of using cloud infrastructure, including greater performance, increased security, and easier management. Understanding the foundations of cloud deployment is critical for developers and companies to ensure a successful deployment process.

One of the most important elements to consider when moving Laravel apps to the cloud is choosing the right cloud service provider. Major cloud computing companies, such as Amazon Web Services (AWS), Microsoft Azure, and Google Cloud Platform (GCP), provide a diverse range of services suited to specific application requirements. Pricing, scalability, security features, and geographical reach may all be used to choose the best cloud provider for a certain Laravel application.

Setting up the infrastructure for the application is a critical stage in cloud deployment. Configuring virtual machines, storage resources, networking components, and security standards are all part of this. Depending on the scope and requirements of the application, deploying Laravel apps frequently entails the creation of virtual servers or the use of serverless computing alternatives. Using solutions such as AWS Elastic Beanstalk, Azure App Service, or Google App Engine can help speed up the deployment process, allowing developers to concentrate on application development rather than infrastructure maintenance.

Containerization has emerged as a popular approach for deploying Laravel applications on the cloud. Technologies like Docker and Kubernetes facilitate the packaging of applications and their dependencies into portable containers, enabling seamless deployment across different cloud environments. Container orchestration tools like Kubernetes help manage the deployment, scaling, and monitoring of containerized applications, ensuring high availability and reliability.

When delivering Laravel apps to the cloud, it is critical to include strong security measures. This includes protecting sensitive data in transit and at rest, enforcing access control regulations, and using encryption mechanisms. Using cloud-native security services like AWS Identity and Access Management (IAM) or Azure Active Directory helps improve the application's overall security posture, by enabling better user management and authentication.

Continuous integration and continuous deployment (CI/CD) pipelines can help to expedite the development workflow and assure the speedy and error-free deployment of Laravel applications. Developers may use integration technologies like Jenkins, GitLab CI/CD, and GitHub Actions to automate testing, build processes, and deployment operations, resulting in a more agile and efficient development cycle. By incorporating automated testing and quality assurance methods into the CI/CD pipeline, developers may detect and fix issues earlier in the development cycle, resulting in more stable and dependable cloud deployment of Laravel apps.

Monitoring and managing the performance of Laravel applications in the cloud is essential to ensure optimal functionality and user experience. Implementing monitoring tools like AWS CloudWatch, Azure Monitor, or Google Cloud Monitoring enables real-time tracking of application metrics, resource utilization, and system health. Proactive monitoring helps detect and resolve performance issues, bottlenecks, and potential failures, ensuring the seamless operation of Laravel applications in the cloud environment.

Cloud Providers Overview

When considering cloud deployment for Laravel applications, understanding the fundamentals of various cloud providers is crucial. Here, we'll provide an overview of the three popular cloud providers—Heroku, Amazon Web Services (AWS), and Google Cloud—to highlight their unique features and benefits.

Amazon Web Services

Amazon Web Services (AWS) is a major participant in the cloud computing sector, providing a complete portfolio of services targeted to developers' and organizations' different demands. With services like Amazon Elastic Compute Cloud (EC2) for virtual server deployment and Amazon RDS for managed database services, AWS provides a scalable and secure platform for hosting Laravel apps.

AWS also provides a large range of tools and services for application monitoring, security, and scalability, allowing developers to create strong and highly available Laravel applications.

While AWS's vast array of services may be intimidating to newcomers, it offers unparalleled flexibility and scalability for complicated application installations.

Heroku

Heroku is well-known for its ease of use and user-friendly UI, making it an excellent choice for developers looking for quick deployment without the headache of complicated setups. Heroku streamlines the deployment process by integrating with Git, allowing developers to focus on application development rather than infrastructure maintenance.

It supports a variety of programming languages, including PHP, making it an excellent alternative for delivering Laravel apps. Heroku's versatility, however, may be limited in comparison to other cloud providers because it abstracts many underlying infrastructure aspects.

Google Cloud

Google Cloud is another prominent cloud platform that is well-known for its performance, dependability, and scalability. Google Cloud, with its global network of data centers and powerful networking capabilities, provides a competitive advantage in terms of speed and accessibility, especially for applications with a global user base.

The Google Cloud platform, which includes Google Compute Engine for virtual machine deployment and Google Cloud SQL for managed database services, offers developers a safe and scalable environment for hosting Laravel apps.

The emphasis on data analytics and machine learning capabilities in Google Cloud increases its attractiveness for developers wishing to integrate modern technology into their apps.

Depending on the needs of the Laravel application, each of these cloud providers has unique characteristics and caters to various use cases.

Consideration of variables like simplicity of usage, scalability, security, and cost may assist developers and companies in selecting the best cloud provider for their Laravel deployment requirements.

Developers may assure the easy deployment and effective operation of Laravel apps by using the capabilities of Heroku, AWS, or Google Cloud, offering ideal user experiences and driving corporate success in the digital world.

Laravel Application Deployment with Vapor

Laravel Vapor is an auto-scaling, serverless Laravel deployment tool powered by AWS Lambda. Manage your Laravel infrastructure with Vapor and fall in love with serverless scalability and simplicity.

Vapor encapsulates the complexities of operating Laravel applications on AWS Lambda, as well as interacting with SQS queues, databases, Redis clusters, networks, CloudFront CDN, and other services.

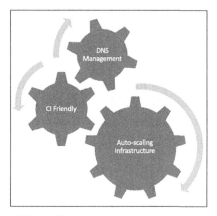

Figure 10.1: *Laravel Vapor features*

Prerequisites of Vapor – PHP 7.3+ and Laravel 6.0+

Installation

In order to deploy through Laravel Vapor it is required to use the Vapor CLI. Run the following commands to install it globally or in each project as:

Global:

```
composer global require laravel/vapor-cli --update-with-dependencies
```

For each Project:

```
composer require laravel/vapor-cli --update-with-dependencies
```

Note: If you install it globally, you do not need to install the CLI for each project.

When the CLI is installed per project, you will most likely need to run it from your project's vendor/bin directory, which is where Composer installs executables. To see all of the available Vapor CLI commands, for example, use the list command:

```
php vendor/bin/vapor list
```

Use the **help** command and the name of the command you want to investigate:

```
php vendor/bin/vapor help deploy
```

Installing the Vapor Core

Every Laravel application that uses Vapor must have the **laravel/vapor-core** package loaded as a dependency. This package includes several Vapor runtime files as well as a service provider that will allow your application to operate on Vapor. Composer may be used to integrate the Vapor Core into your project:

```
composer require laravel/vapor-core --update-with-dependencies
```

Installing the Vapor Dashboard

You may also wish to install the **laravel/vapor-ui** package. This package adds a lovely dashboard to your application that allows you to monitor logs and unsuccessful queue processes. After you deploy your app to Vapor, the dashboard will be accessible via the **/vapor-ui** URI. Composer may be used to install the Vapor UI dashboard package in your project:

```
composer require laravel/vapor-ui
```

You may use the **vapor-ui:install** Artisan command to publish its assets:

```
php artisan vapor-ui:install
```

The dashboard will be accessible using the **/vapor-ui** URI.

Dashboard Authorization

At the **/vapor-ui** URI, Vapor UI offers a dashboard. There is a **gate** function in your **app/Providers/VaporUiServiceProvider.php** file that regulates access to the Vapor UI dashboard. All visitors are limited by default. To grant access to your Vapor UI dashboard, you should alter this **gate** as needed:

```
protected function gate()
{
    Gate::define('viewVaporUI', function ($user = null) {

        return in_array(optional($user)->email, [

            'abc@example.com',

        ]);

    });
}
```

Environment

All of your deployments and command executions are saved in environments. Every project may have as many environments as it requires.

Typically, you will have a **production** environment and a **staging** environment for testing your application. However, don't be scared to set up other environments for testing new features without interfering with your primary staging environment.

The **env** Vapor CLI tool may be used to build environments:

```
vapor env my-environment
```

This command will add a new environment entry to your project's **vapor.yml** file, ready for deployment:

```
id: 3
name: vapor-laravel-app
environments:
    production:
        build:
            - 'composer install --no-dev'
    my-environment:
        build:
            - 'composer install --no-dev'
```

Vapor allows Docker image deployments in addition to native runtimes. When building an environment, use the **--docker** option to specify that it should utilize a Docker image runtime rather than the default Vapor runtime.

```
vapor env my-environment --docker
```

This command will establish a new environment called **my-environment.Dockerfile** file at the root directory of your application.

The open command in the Vapor CLI may be used to open environments in your default browser:

```
vapor open my-environment
```

Vapor CLI utilizes the staging environment by default when performing a command:

vapor open // Opens the `staging` environment in default browser

vapor open production // Opens the `production` environment in default browser

However, you may alter the default environment for your project by defining a default-environment option in your application's **vapor.yml** file:

```
id: 3
name: vapor-laravel-app
default-environment: production
environments:
    production:
        build:
            - 'composer install --no-dev'
    my-environment:
        build:
            - 'composer install --no-dev'
```

Environment Variables

Each environment comprises a collection of environment variables that, like the variables in your application's local **.env** file, offer critical information to your program during execution.

All of the environment variables that are injected by Vapor, along with their **env()** values, are listed in the following table:

.env Value	**env() Value**
APP_ENV	Environment name
APP_DEBUG	FALSE
APP_LOG_LEVEL	Debug
APP_URL	Vanity domain, or custom domain if exists

ASSET_URL	CloudFront
AWS_BUCKET	Storage resource if exists
BROADCAST_DRIVER	Pusher
CACHE_DRIVER	DynamoDB, or cache (Redis) resource if exists
DB_*	Database (MySQL, Postgresql, etc) resource if exists
DYNAMODB_CACHE_TABLE	**vapor_cache**
FILESYSTEM_DISK	S3
FILESYSTEM_DRIVER	S3
FILESYSTEM_CLOUD	S3
LOG_CHANNEL	Stderr
MAIL_DRIVER	LOG, but SES for environments with the name **production**
MAIL_MAILER	LOG, but SES for environments with the name **production**
MAIL_FROM_ADDRESS	**hello@example.com** or **hello@custom-domain.com** if exists
MAIL_FROM_NAME	**your_project_name**

MIX_URL	CloudFront
QUEUE_ CONNECTION	SQS
SCHEDULE_CACHE_ DRIVER	DynamoDB
SESSION_DRIVER	Cookie

Table 10.1: Environment Variables injected by Vapor on the environment

When you manage your environment with Vapor CLI or Vapor UI, you will not see these environment variables, and any variables you explicitly set will override Vapor's automatically injected variables.

Deployment

Deployments can only be started via the Vapor CLI. Vapor will perform the build steps of your **vapor.yml** file on the local computer that the deployment is executing on during deployment. This might be your own computer or a continuous integration platform.

To begin a deployment, use the `deploy` CLI command from your application's root directory.

```
vapor deploy production
```

Hooks

You may specify build hooks for an environment in your **vapor.yml** file by utilizing the **build** keyword. These instructions are run on the local system where the deployment is taking place and may be used to prepare your application for deployment. During deployment, your application is constructed under a temporary **.vapor** directory established by the CLI, and all of your **build** instructions are executed within that directory:

```
id: 4
name: vapor-app
environments:
```

```
production:
  memory: 1024
  database: vapor-app
  cache: vapor-cache
  build:
    - 'composer install --no-dev'
    - 'php artisan event:cache'

  deploy:
    - 'php artisan migrate --force'
```

You may specify deployment hooks for an environment in your **vapor.yml** file by using the deploy key. These commands are run on the deployed environment before it is made available to the public. The deployment will not be activated if any of these instructions fail:

```
id: 4
name: vapor-app
environments:
  production:
    memory: 1024
    database: vapor-app
    cache: vapor-cache
    build:
      - 'composer install --no-dev'
      - 'php artisan event:cache'

    deploy:
      - 'php artisan migrate --force'
```

When a deployment hook fails, you may see the output / logs via the deployment detail tab in the Vapor UI.

Also, if you use the **vapor deploy** command to deploy your application, the CLI output will include the unsuccessful hook output. Of course, you may inspect the output at any moment by utilizing the **hook:output** for output:

```
vapor hook:output {DEPLOYMENT_HOOK_ID}
```

Using the **hook:log** command, you may examine the logs connected with the unsuccessful:

```
vapor hook:log {DEPLOYMENT_HOOK_ID}
```

Development

To return binary replies from your Vapor application, such as PDF downloads, your HTTP response should contain the **X-Vapor-Base64-Encode** header:

```
return $response->withHeaders([

    'X-Vapor-Base64-Encode' => 'True',

]);
```

Configure OpenSSL

OpenSSL stands out as a widely employed open-source software library, furnishing an array of cryptographic functions and protocols. In the realm of Laravel applications or any web-based application, OpenSSL assumes a pivotal role in safeguarding the security of both data transmission and storage.

Here are some fundamental aspects of OpenSSL in the context of a Laravel application:

- **Encryption and Decryption:** OpenSSL empowers the encryption and decryption of data, particularly crucial for securing sensitive information, such as user credentials, personal data, and financial transactions. In the Laravel framework, OpenSSL is harnessed to establish secure communication through HTTPS (HTTP Secure), encrypting data during transmission.

- **SSL/TLS Protocols**: OpenSSL lends support to various SSL (Secure Sockets Layer) and TLS (Transport Layer Security) protocols, vital for securing communication between a web server and a client (such as a web browser). These protocols guarantee that the data exchanged between the client and the server remains encrypted, shielding it from unauthorized access.

- **Digital Signatures**: Offering functions for creating and verifying digital signatures, OpenSSL plays a key role in ensuring the integrity and authenticity of data. In Laravel, digital signatures can be employed to authenticate data received from clients or other servers.

- **Certificate Handling**: SSL/TLS certificates constitute a critical component of secure web communication. OpenSSL simplifies the generation, management, and verification of SSL/TLS certificates. Laravel applications frequently leverage OpenSSL for SSL certificate management, establishing secure connections.

- **Hashing and Message Digests**: OpenSSL incorporates cryptographic hash functions that Laravel can utilize for tasks such as hashing passwords or generating message digests. Hashing is pivotal for securely storing passwords and ensuring data integrity.

OpenSSL equips developers with indispensable tools for encryption, decryption, digital signatures, and certificate management, bolstering the overall security of the application and its interactions with users and other services.

To utilize OpenSSL functions like **openssl_pkey_new**, you must first build an **openssl.cnf** configuration file and tell Vapor to load it using the **OPENSSL_CONF** environment variable. For example, this environment variable instructs Vapor to import an **openssl.cnf** file from your project's root:

```
OPENSSL_CONF="/var/task/openssl.cnf"
```

Let's look at the sample **openssl.cnf** file:

```
dir = certificates


[ ca ]
default_ca = CA_default


[ CA_default ]
serial = $dir/serial
database = $dir/index.txt
new_certs_dir = $dir/newcerts
```

```
certificate   = $dir/cacert.pem
private_key = $dir/private/cakey.pem
default_days = 36500
default_md   = sha256
preserve = no
email_in_dn   = no
nameopt = default_ca
certopt = default_ca
policy = policy_match

[ policy_match ]
commonName = supplied
countryName = optional
stateOrProvinceName = optional
organizationName = optional
organizationalUnitName = optional
emailAddress = optional

[ req ]
default_bits = 2048
default_keyfile = priv.pem
default_md = sha256
distinguished_name = req_distinguished_name
req_extensions = v3_req
encyrpt_key = no

[ req_distinguished_name ]

[ v3_ca ]
basicConstraints = CA:TRUE
subjectKeyIdentifier = hash
authorityKeyIdentifier = keyid:always,issuer:always
```

```
[ v3_req ]
basicConstraints = CA:FALSE
subjectKeyIdentifier = hash
Source : docs.vapor.build
```

You can dispatch tasks in typical Laravel apps that will be run when the HTTP response is given to the browser:

```
Route::get('/', function () {
    dispatch(function () {
        Mail::to(abc@example.com')->send(new WelcomeMessage);
    })->afterResponse();

    return view('home');
});
```

When utilizing Vapor, we always recommend dispatching jobs to your queue workers. Because Vapor cannot run a task after receiving a response from the browser, attempting to do so will make your application look slower to the end user.

Domains

When you use Vapor, each environment is assigned a unique vanity domain that you may use to access the environment once it has been deployed. However, bear in mind that vanity domains are exclusively for development purposes, and Vapor automatically inserts *no-index* headers to replies from these URLs to prevent search engines from indexing them.

Furthermore, even while an application is in maintenance mode, these vanity domains will continue to work, allowing you to test your environment before disabling maintenance mode and restoring general access.

While vanity domains might be beneficial during the development phase, they should not be used in a production setting or shared with the public. Instead, it is recommended to utilize your own custom code.

You may add a domain that you own to Vapor via the domain screen or the domain CLI command. Even if you intend to serve your application via a subdomain, always add the root domain when adding a domain to Vapor:

```
vapor domain example.com
```

To inspect the specifics of your Vapor domains using the Vapor UI or the **domain:list** CLI command:

```
vapor domain:list
```

DNS Records

When you add a domain to Vapor, you'll be given nameservers to enter into your domain registrar's nameserver settings page. This will make Vapor the entity in charge of the domain's DNS records. Vapor may also automatically add and remove DNS records from the domain as required.

If you wish to handle your DNS records independently, acquiring a certificate or connecting the domain to an environment will require manually creating DNS records through your domain registrar.

Custom Records

If you've elected to let Vapor maintain your DNS records, you may add, edit, or delete DNS records whenever you want. Vapor allows you to manage your DNS records in two ways: through the Vapor UI's domain information panel or using the Vapor CLI. You may use the record command to generate a DNS record using the Vapor CLI:

```
vapor record example.com A www 192.168.1.1
```

```
vapor record example.com A @ 192.168.1.1
```

```
vapor record example.com CNAME foo another-example.com
```

```
vapor record example.com MX foo "10 example.com,20 example2.com"
```

Source : docs.vapor.build

You may use the **record:delete** command to remove a record using the Vapor CLI command to delete:

```
vapor record:delete example.com A www
```

SSL Certificates

A valid SSL certificate is required before adding a domain to an existing Vapor environment. Vapor provides free, automated SSL certificate renewals for your Vapor environment using AWS Certificate Manager.

Users often select the *us-east-1* area for their certificate, which is the necessary certificate region for all API Gateway 1.0 setups. Environments employing API Gateway 2.0 or Application Load Balancers, on the other hand, require a certificate in the same area as the project.

You may generate a certificate using the domain screen in the Vapor UI or the **cert** CLI command:

```
vapor cert example.com
```

The validity status of your certificates may be seen using the Vapor UI or by using the **cert:list** command CLI command list:

```
vapor cert:list example.com
```

If you wish to destroy an old certificate that is no longer associated with an environment, use the domain information page in the Vapor UI or the **cert:delete** CLI command. Vapor will offer you to pick the individual certificate you wish to destroy for the provided domain when you execute the command:

```
vapor cert:delete example.com
```

Add Domain to Environment

Once your domain has a valid SSL certificate, you may use the **domain** configuration option in your application's **vapor.yml** file to connect it to your environment. You do not need to add the www subdomain when linking a domain to an environment:

```
id: 3
name: vapor-laravel-app
environments:
    production:


        domain: example.com
        build:
            - 'composer install --no-dev'
```

Vapor will automatically set up the environment to handle requests from this domain upon deployment. However, because of the nature of AWS CloudFront, custom domains sometimes take 30-45 minutes to completely activate. So, don't be concerned if your custom domain isn't instantly available after deployment.

Vapor lets you associate many domains with a single project. Make sure you have a valid certificate for each of the domains before proceeding. Then, change the **vapor.yml** file in your application to add each domain:

```
id: 3
name: vapor-laravel-app
environments:
    production:
        domain:
            - example1.com
            - example2.com
        build:
            - 'composer install --no-dev'
```

As long as you have a valid certificate for the parent domain, you can specify that a domain should enable wildcard subdomains. To associate a wildcard domain with an environment, use * as the subdomain:

```
id: 3
name: vapor-laravel-app
environments:
    production:
        domain: '*.example.com'
        build:
            - 'composer install --no-dev'
```

Multi-Level Subdomains

Vapor supports multiple-level subdomains, such as **v1.api.example.com**. To use this capability, a certificate that specifically covers the whole multi-level subdomain must be obtained.

The certificate may be obtained by using the Vapor CLI:

```
vapor cert v1.api.example.com
```

A certificate for a multi-level subdomain may also be obtained via the Vapor domains dashboard by specifying the multi-level subdomain as either the Domain Name or any of the Alternative Names in the Advanced Settings when requesting a certificate.

When the certificate is granted, you may access your application from your multi-level subdomain by adding it to the **domain** section of your **vapor.yml** configuration file and doing a complete deployment via the Vapor CLI:

```
id: 3
name: vapor-laravel-app
environments:
    production:
        domain: 'v1.api.example.com'
        build:
            - 'composer install --no-dev'
```

Troubleshooting

While leveraging Vapor to drive your Laravel applications can significantly enhance load speeds, it's important to address potential performance issues stemming from misconfigured infrastructure.

This section delves into a series of key techniques for optimizing Vapor infrastructure, with the aim of bolstering the speed of your Laravel applications. Before we delve into these techniques, it's crucial to consider the following points:

- **Prioritize application optimization:** Boosting your application's speed might eliminate the need for any modifications to the infrastructure. Identify and address performance bottlenecks within the application by implementing fundamental strategies such as caching, queuing, or optimizing database queries.

Be mindful of the potential impact on your AWS expenses: Implementing changes to your Vapor environment by adding or adjusting resources could lead to an increase in your AWS bill.

- **Utilizing fixed-capacity databases:**

Serverless databases are designed to scale automatically, without a predefined limit on RAM or disk space. However, AWS's method of *auto-scaling* can lead to brief delays known as cold starts whenever additional database resources are needed within your environment.

To mitigate this challenge, consider implementing *fixed-capacity* databases that come with pre-allocated resources. You can easily create these databases using either the Vapor UI or the dedicated database CLI command.

- **Opting API Gateway v2 over API Gateway v1 for improved performance:**

Transitioning from API Gateway v1 to API Gateway v2 can lead to a significant 50% decrease in query latency for your application. However, it's important to note that API Gateway v2 operates on a regional basis, potentially impacting clients located in distant regions. Furthermore, certain functionalities like Vapor's controlled Firewall may not be accessible with this switch.

To integrate API Gateway 2.0, simply include gateway-version: 2 in the settings of your environment's **vapor.yml** file.

Conclusion

The chapter, *Deploying Laravel: A Comprehensive Guide*, delves into the crucial process of deploying a Laravel application to the cloud. It begins by discussing the fundamentals of cloud deployment, emphasizing the importance of choosing the right cloud service provider, setting up infrastructure, and prioritizing security. The chapter highlights the significance of containerization, continuous integration, and continuous deployment (CI/CD) pipelines, as well as monitoring and managing performance in the cloud.

Furthermore, the chapter provides an insightful overview of three major cloud providers: Heroku, Amazon Web Services (AWS), and Google Cloud, analyzing their unique features and benefits for hosting Laravel applications. The discussion sheds light on the distinctive offerings and considerations involved in selecting a cloud provider.

The focal point of the chapter is the deployment of Laravel applications with Laravel Vapor, an auto-scaling, serverless Laravel deployment tool powered by AWS Lambda. The chapter walks through the prerequisites, installation, and configuration process, including setting up environments, handling environment variables, deploying applications, and managing domains. It also provides detailed instructions and code snippets to facilitate a smooth deployment process.

Notably, the chapter covers essential topics such as hooks, development considerations, customizing OpenSSL, configuring domains, managing DNS records, and handling SSL certificates. It concludes with a comprehensive section on troubleshooting common performance issues and optimizing the infrastructure for enhanced application speed, all while being mindful of potential impacts on AWS expenses.

Throughout the chapter, emphasis is placed on practical implementation, with step-by-step instructions and real-world scenarios to guide readers through the complexities of deploying Laravel applications to the cloud. The provided insights and best practices serve as valuable resources for developers and organizations seeking efficient and reliable deployment solutions for their Laravel applications.

Points to Remember

- Understand the significance of cloud deployment, including choosing the right cloud service provider, setting up infrastructure, prioritizing security, and implementing containerization for seamless deployment across different cloud environments.

- Evaluate the unique features and benefits of major cloud providers such as Heroku, AWS, and Google Cloud, considering factors like ease of use, scalability, security, and geographical reach, to ensure the best fit for your Laravel application deployment needs.

- Explore the capabilities of Laravel Vapor, an auto-scaling, serverless Laravel deployment tool powered by AWS Lambda, to simplify the deployment process. Pay attention to the prerequisites, installation steps, and configurations required for a successful deployment.

- Learn how to set up and manage environments, handle environment variables, and utilize the Vapor CLI tool effectively for streamlined deployment operations. Understand the significance of defining and managing multiple environments, including production and staging, to ensure smooth testing and development processes.

- Explore the management of domains, including setting up vanity domains for development purposes, configuring DNS records, handling SSL certificates, and associating multiple domains with a single project. Ensure proper domain configuration for seamless access and usage of the Laravel application.

- Be aware of common performance issues and optimization techniques for the Vapor infrastructure. Prioritize application optimization, consider the impact on AWS expenses, and implement strategies such as fixed-capacity databases and API Gateway v2 for improved performance and reduced latency.

- Emphasize the importance of continuous monitoring and security measures for ensuring optimal functionality and data protection in the cloud environment. Implement best practices for securing sensitive data, enforcing access control regulations, and utilizing cloud-native security services for enhanced application security.

- Understand the significance of implementing CI/CD pipelines for automating testing, build processes, and deployment operations. Ensure early detection and resolution of issues during the development cycle, leading to more stable and reliable cloud deployment of Laravel applications.

Index

A

access tokens
  about 175
  client 175, 176
  JSON API 176
  routes, protecting 178
  scope 180
actions
  securing, with middleware 143
advanced join 100
advanced subqueries 115, 116
advanced where 100
aggregate 101
Amazon Web Services (AWS) 231
API authentication services 124
Application Programming
      Interface (API) 157

Artisan
  about 18
  commands 18
  history 18
Artisan, commands
  custom schedule job 22
  frequent repeating jobs 20
  help command 19
  isolatable command 22, 23
  list command 19
  overlapping job 22
  scheduling command 19
  specific day job 21
  specific time weekly 21
  version command 19
  weekly repeating job 21
auth directive 74, 75
authentication guards
  about 136, 137
  closure request guard 137, 138

authentication method
  about 140
  user id, authenticating 142
  user instance, authenticating 141
  user once, authenticating 142
authorization policies and gates
  authentication guards 136, 137
  authentication method 140
  implementing 132
  password management 134
  user session, invalidating 139
  user session knowledge 140
  user sessions, invalidating 133, 134

B

Blade
  about 79
  components 81
  data 79, 80
  HTML entity encoding 80
  layouts 84, 85
  rendering Blade fragments 87, 88
  rendering Blade template 86
broadcast notification
  about 221-223
  events 224, 225

C

caching 51
class dependency management 3
client 175
closure request guard 137, 138
cloud deployment
  fundamentals 230, 231
cloud providers
  Amazon Web Services (AWS) 231
  Google Cloud 232
  Heroku 232
  overview 231
collections 111, 112

components
  about 81
  data passing 83, 84
  rendering component 82
Composer
  installing 14
  installing, on Mac 14
  installing, on Windows 16
composite primary key 108
conditional directives
  about 72, 73
  if statement 73
conditional relationships 167, 168
constructor injection 67
controller actions 70
controllers
  about 48, 49, 64, 65
  constructor injection 67
  method injection 68
  resource controllers 65, 66
cross-origin resource
     sharing (CORS) 50
CRUD model operations 116, 117
cursor 114, 115
custom authentication
     and registration logic
  about 125
  HTTP authentication 125, 126
  stateless HTTP authentication 126
  user provider 127
custom records 245
custom symfony message 221
custom template
  about 217, 218
  raw data, handling 219

D

data and view 54
database connection 110

database migration
  about 92, 93
  primary key 93, 94
  timestamps 94, 95
data passing 83, 84
data wrapping 163-167
debugging 202, 203
design principles, MVC architecture
        pattern
  cohesion 29
  components 30
  coupling 30
  flexibility 29
  reusability 29
directives
  about 71, 72
  auth directive 74, 75
  conditional directives 72, 73
  loops 76, 77
  once directive 78, 79
  switch directive 73, 74
DNS records 245
domains
  about 244
  multi-level subdomain 248

E

Eloquent
  about 91, 92
  database migration 92, 93
  events 95, 96
Eloquent operations
  about 102
  CRUD model operations 116, 117
  events 118, 119, 120
  model class 103
  model conventions 104
  retrieval model 110
Eloquent ORM
  about 3
  authentication 5

authorization 5
  mail service 4
  message queue system 4
  scheduling 4
  URL routing configuration 4
email component
  customizing 215-217
  custom template 217-219
environment variables 237-239

F

fallback routes 41
features, MVC architecture design
        pattern
  extensibility 32
  maintainability 32
  Search Engine Optimization (SEO) 31
  Simultaneous Development 32
  Test Driven Development (TDD) 32
file upload testing 200-202
first view 53, 54
flashed session data 70, 71

G

generate notification 206
Google Cloud 232

H

Heroku 232
Homebrew
  used, for installing Mac 14, 15
homogeneous primary key 106, 107
hooks 239-241
HTML entity encoding 80
HTTP authentication 125, 126
HTTP tests
  about 193
  request headers, customizing 194
  request, making 193, 194

I

if statement 73
Installer
   used, for installing Laravel 17
   used, for installing Mac 15, 16

J

joins 99
   advanced join 100
   left join 99
JSON API
   about 176
   DELETE 178
   GET 176
   POST 177
   PUT 177, 178

L

lang directory 11
Laravel
   about 2
   core concept 24, 25
   installing 17
   installing, on Linux 17
   installing, on Mac 17
   installing, on Windows 17
   installing, via Composer
        Create-Project 18
   installing, via Installer 17
   installing, via PHP serve 18
   preference 2
Laravel 10 version
   about 8
   upgrading 8
Laravel 10 version, dependencies
   about 8, 9
   database expressions 10
   Eloquent model 10
   minimum stability 9

public path binding 9
redis cache tags 10
testing 11
Laravel application
   deploying, with Vapor 233
   environment test, setting up 186, 187
   lifecycle test 187
   testing techniques 186
   Vapor core, installing 234
   Vapor, installing 233, 234
Laravel application, lifecycle test
   parallel tests, executing 189-192
   tests, creating 187, 188
   tests, reporting 192
   tests, running 189
Laravel built-in authentication system
   about 123
   API authentication services 124
   passport 124, 125
   Sanctum 125
Laravel community 3
Laravel development environment
   Composer, installing 14
   installation 11
   Laravel, installing 17
   PHP, installing 11
   setting up 11
Laravel features
   about 5
   database seeding 5
   localization 6
Laravel Passport
   about 170
   composer package manager,
        installing 171
   configuring 172
   driver option, setting up 172
Laravel Passport, configuration
   default models, overriding 173, 174
   routes, overriding 174, 175
   token lifetimes 172, 173

layouts
  about 84, 85
  template inheritance 85, 86
left join 99
Linux
  used, for installing Laravel 17
localization 6
loops 76, 77

M

Mac
  installing, via Homebrew 14, 15
  installing, via Installer 15, 16
  used, for installing Composer 14
  used, for installing Laravel 17
  used, for installing PHP 11, 12
mail notification
  about 214, 215
  custom symfony message 221
  email component,
      customizing 215-217
  tags and metadata 220, 221
method injection 68
middleware
  about 47, 143-145
  assigning, to routes 146-148
  used, for securing routes
      and actions 142, 143
middleware groups
  about 148, 149
  parameters 151, 152
  sorting 150
  terminable middleware 152, 154
model class 103
model conventions
  about 104
  database connection 110
  primary key 105
  table name 105
  ULID key 108, 109
  UUID key 108, 109

MVC architecture
  about 2
  components 27
  history 27
  overview 26
MVC architecture design pattern
  about 30
  controller 34
  key features 31
  models 33
  views 33
MVC architecture pattern
  about 28, 29
  design principles 29

N

named routes 69, 70
nested views directories 53

O

once directive 78, 79
OpenSSL
  configuring 242
  fundamental aspects 241
optional parameter 42

P

passport 124, 125
password management
  about 134
  configuring 134
  routing 134, 135
pessimistic locking 102
PHP
  installing 11
  installing, on Mac 11, 12
  installing, on Windows 12-14
primary key
  about 93, 94, 105
  composite primary key 108
  homogeneous primary key 106, 107

Q

Query Builder
  about 97
  advanced where 100
  aggregate 101
  joins 99
  pessimistic locking 102
  query cache 102
  raw expression 101
  selects 97, 98
query cache 102
queue connection
  about 210, 211
  channel 211-213
  on-demand notification 213

R

rational expression 43
raw expression 101
redirect
  about 69
  controller actions 70
  flashed session data 70, 71
  named routes 69, 70
  redirect helper 69
redirect helper 69
redirect routes 40
regular expression constraint 43
regular expression (Regex) 43-46
relationships 162
rendering Blade fragments 87, 88
rendering Blade template 86
rendering component 82
Representational State
        Transfer (REST) 157
request headers
  authentication 196, 197
  cookies 195
  customizing 194

debugging response 198, 199
  exception handling 200
resource controllers 65, 66
resource response 169
resources
  about 157-161
  writing 161, 162
retrieval model
  about 110
  advanced subqueries 115, 116
  chunk result 112, 113
  chunk, with lazy collection 113, 114
  collections 111, 112
  cursor 114, 115
route groups 46, 47
route list 40, 41
route parameter 41, 42
route prefix 49, 50
router methods 39
routers
  about 37
  caching 51
  controllers 48, 49
  cross-origin resource
        sharing (CORS) 50
  middleware 47
  optional parameter 42
  regular expression constraint 43
  regular expression (Regex) 44-46
  route groups 46, 47
  route parameter 41, 42
  route prefix 49, 50
  router methods 39
  routes directory 38
  subdomain routing 49
routers types
  about 39
  fallback routes 41
  redirect routes 40
  route list 40, 41
  view routes 40

routes
  access token 180
  middleware 179
  middleware, assigning 146-148
  protecting 178
  securing, with middleware 143
routes directory 38

S

Sanctum 125
scope
  checking 182, 183
  default function 181
  defining 180, 182
Search Engine Optimization (SEO)
  about 31
  need for 31
  principles 31, 32
selects 97, 98
send notification
  about 206, 207
  delaying 209
  delivery channels 207
  queue connection 210, 211
  queuing 208, 209
sharedLock method 102
Simple Object Access
        Protocol (SOAP) 157
SSL certificate 246
stateless HTTP authentication 126
subdomain routing 49
switch directive 73, 74

T

table name 105
template inheritance 85, 86
Test Driven Development (TDD) 32
timestamps 94, 95
translation strings
  JSON files 6-8
  lang directory 6

troubleshooting
  about 249
  API Gateway v2, opting 249
  application optimization,
        prioritizing 249
  fixed-capacity databases,
        utilizing 249

U

ULID key 108, 109
user provider
  about 127-129
  authenticatable contract 131, 132
  contract 129, 130
user session
  invalidating 139
user session knowledge 140
UUID key 108, 109

V

Vapor
  about 233
  used, for deploying Laravel
        application 233
Vapor core
  custom records 245
  dashboard authorization 235
  dashboard, installing 234
  deployment 239
  development 241
  DNS records 245
  domain, adding
        to environment 246, 247
  domains 244, 245
  environment 235-237
  hooks 239-241
  installing 234
  OpenSSL, configuring 241-244
  SSL certificate 246

view composers
  about 56-59
  multiple views 59, 60
view creators 56, 60
view optimization 60, 61
view routes 40
views
  about 51
  creating 52, 53
  data and view 54
  data sharing 55
  extension 53
  first view 53, 54
  nested views directories 53
  view optimization 60, 61

W

Windows
  used, for installing Composer 16
  used, for installing Laravel 17
  used, for installing PHP 12-14

Made in the USA
Coppell, TX
09 March 2025

46856510R00155